Do-it Yourself

BASICS

Save Money • Solve Problems • Improve Your Home

THE BASICS EVERYONE CAN MASTER

Reader's digest

The Reader's Digest Association, Inc.
New York, NY/Montreal

Do-It Yourself Basics

Publisher Nancy Taylor
**Content Management, Design
and Page Layout** Elizabeth Tunnicliffe
Cover Design George McKeon
Manufacturing Manager John L. Cassidy
Proofreader Judy Arginteanu

Text, photography and illustrations for *Do-It Yourself Basics* are based on articles previously published in *The Family Handyman* magazine (2915 Commers Dr., Suite 700, Eagan, MN 55121, familyhandyman.com). For information on advertising in *The Family Handyman* magazine, call (646) 518-4231.

Do-It Yourself Basics is published by Trusted Media Brands, Inc. ©2017

Family Handyman ISBN: 978-1-62145-353-6

Reader's Digest ISBN: 978-1-62145-375-8

Address any comments to:
feedback@familyhandyman.com

A Note to Our Readers
All do-it-yourself activities involve a degree of risk. Skills, materials, tools and site conditions vary widely. Although the editors have made every effort to ensure accuracy, the reader remains responsible for the selection and use of tools, materials and methods. Always obey local codes and laws, follow manufacturer instructions and observe safety precautions.

Pricing
Professional services and supplies can vary widely depending on the market. Those listed are average costs and are just a guide to cost savings.

The Family Handyman

Editor in Chief Gary Wentz
Senior Editor Travis Larson
Associate and Contributing Editors Mary Flanagan, Jeff Gorton, Mark Petersen, Jason White
Digital Content Editor Andrew Zoeliner
Managing Editor Donna Bierbach
Contributing Copy Editor Peggy Parker
Art Directors Vern Johnson, Marcia Roepke
Production Artist Mary Schwender
Photographer Tom Fenenga
Contributing Editors Elisa Bernick, Spike Carlsen, Ken Collier, Rick Muscoplat, David Radtke
Lead Carpenter Josh Risberg
Editorial Services Associate Peggy McDermott

Trusted Media Brands, Inc.

President & Chief Executive Officer
Bonnie Kintzer

PRINTED IN CHINA

2 3 4 5 6 7 8 9 10

Safety first–always!

Tackling home improvement projects and repairs can be endlessly rewarding.
But as most of us know, with the rewards come risks.
The good news is, armed with the right knowledge, tools and procedures, homeowners
can minimize risk. As you go about your projects and repairs, stay alert for these hazards:

Aluminum wiring

Aluminum wiring, installed in about 7 million homes between 1965 and 1973, requires special techniques and materials to make safe connections. This wiring is dull gray, not the dull orange characteristic of copper. Hire a licensed electrician certified to work with it. For more information go to cpsc.gov and search for "aluminum wiring."

Spontaneous combustion

Rags saturated with oil finishes like Danish oil and linseed oil, and oil-based paints and stains can spontaneously combust if left bunched up. Always dry them outdoors, spread out loosely. When the oil has thoroughly dried, you can safely throw them in the trash.

Vision and hearing protection

Safety glasses or goggles should be worn whenever you're working on DIY projects that involve chemicals, dust and anything that could shatter or chip off and hit your eye. Sounds louder than 80 decibels (dB) are considered potentially dangerous. Sound levels from a lawn mower can be 90 dB, and shop tools and chain saws can be 90 to 100 dB.

Lead paint

If your home was built before 1979, it may contain lead paint, which is a serious health hazard, especially for children 6 and under. Take precautions when you scrape or remove it. Contact your public health department for detailed safety information or call (800) 424-LEAD (5323) to receive an information pamphlet. Or visit epa.gov/lead.

Buried utilities

A few days before you dig in your yard, have your underground water, gas and electrical lines marked. Just call 811 or go to call811.com.

Smoke and carbon monoxide (CO) alarms

The risk of dying in reported home structure fires is cut in half in homes with working smoke alarms. Test your smoke alarms every month, replace batteries as necessary and replace units that are more than 10 years old. As you make your home more energy-efficient and airtight, existing ducts and chimneys can't always successfully vent combustion gases, including potentially deadly carbon monoxide (CO). Install a UL-listed CO detector, and test your CO and smoke alarms at the same time.

Five-gallon buckets and window covering cords

From 1996 to 1999, 58 children under age 5 drowned in 5-gallon buckets. Always store them upside down and store ones containing liquid with the covers securely snapped.

According to Parents for Window Blind Safety, 599 children have been seriously injured or killed in the United States since 1986 after becoming entangled in looped window treatment cords. For more information, visit pfwbs.org or cpsc.gov.

Working up high

If you have to get up on your roof to do a repair or installation, always install roof brackets and wear a roof harness.

Asbestos

Texture sprayed on ceilings before 1978, adhesives and tiles for vinyl and asphalt floors before 1980, and vermiculite insulation (with gray granules) all may contain asbestos. Other building materials, made between 1940 and 1980, could also contain asbestos. If you suspect that materials you're removing or working around contain asbestos, contact your health department or visit epa.gov/asbestos for information.

➤ For additional information about home safety, visit mysafehome.org.
This site offers helpful information about dozens of home safety issues.

Contents

Master Tools

Master the hammer

➤ **Which weight?** A 16-oz. hammer is right for most jobs. Avoid hammers with a jagged "waffle" texture on the striking face. When you miss a nail, they do ugly things to surfaces—or your thumb.

➤ **Style** The basic household hammer is a curved claw but consider a versatile rip claw. When swung backwards it can dig holes, split wood and help break up stuff.

➤ **Nailing** Grip hammer near the end, lightly but firmly. Keeping wrist straight, let the hammer fall naturally, aided by shoulder and upper arm. Hammer the nail to within 1/8 in. of surface; countersink the head with nail set. To use a nail set, position its point over the head of the nail and strike the top with a hammer. Fill the hole with wood putty. (A nail set is a punch-shaped tool designed to sink, or set, nails beneath the surface of the wood.)

NAIL SET

➤ **Pull sideways** The usual way to pull a nail is to lever the claw straight up. But when a nail won't budge, yank the handle to the side. That puts the pivot point closer to the nail for more pulling power.

➤ **Pull against a block** A small block under the claw does two things: It protects the surface beneath it and provides more pulling power, especially after the nail is partially removed.

> **CAUTION:** Wear goggles; a miss-hit can send a nail flying.

RIP CLAW

CURVED CLAW

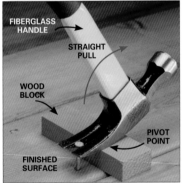

SIDE PULL

UNFINISHED SURFACE

PIVOT POINT

FIBERGLASS HANDLE

STRAIGHT PULL

WOOD BLOCK

PIVOT POINT

FINISHED SURFACE

pro tips!

➤ Holding a small nail or brad when you start is difficult. Stick the nail through one end of a folded sheet of stiff paper. Using the paper as a holder, drive in the nail. Then before seating, tear the paper away.

Drive screws like a pro

➤ **Style** A screwdriver should have a comfortable nonslip handle and a crisply machined blade tip.

➤ **Size** The blade should be the same width as the screwhead and should fit the slot snugly. If too large, the blade may not fit the slot and can damage surrounding surface; if too small, the blade may slip and damage the slot.

➤ **Drill before you drive** In most cases, you can drive construction screws without drilling a hole. If you are having trouble, use an awl to make a pilot hole in wood. For larger screws and masonry, grab a drill bit that's slightly smaller than the diameter of the screw. You'll also avoid splitting the wood as the screw sinks in.

➤ **Choose better screws** Phillips-head screws are a lot easier to drive than screws with a single slot. But when it comes to avoiding cam-out, some are even better—"square-drive" screws, and Torx. Avoid traditional wood screws; they simply don't penetrate wood as easily as modern "construction" screws that have sharper tips.

➤ **Push hard, really hard** Pressure is the best prevention for cam-out. With enough pressure behind it, the blade simply can't slip out of the screwhead's slot.

➤ **For speed** A small electric screwdriver speeds many tasks, especially appliance and electronics repairs. Use a larger model or a drill equipped with screwdriver bit for heavy jobs.

pro tips!

➤ Special screwdrivers make it easier to install screws in awkward places. Use a stubby or an off-set screwdriver where space is limited.

➤ **Drive screws at an angle** "Toe screwing" takes some practice. It allows you to make connections you otherwise couldn't and to hide screws under boards where they won't be seen (under a deck railing as shown here, for example). To make it easier, drill a pilot hole before driving. Or try it without a pilot hole, using this two-step technique.

1. Bore straight into the surface with a drill bit that's slightly smaller than the screw you'll use.

STRAIGHT STARTER HOLE

2. When you've drilled about 1/8 in. into the wood, keep the bit spinning while you shift the drill to a sharp angle.

SHIFT TO SHARP ANGLE

 ➤ **Standard blade**

 ➤ **Phillips blade**

 ➤ **Square-drive**

 ➤ **Torx blade**

CAUTION: Never use slotted-head drivers for Phillips-head screws.

Master your drill

➤ An electric drill is easy to use even for a beginner. While its primary purpose is boring holes, a power drill can also drive screws, sand and polish surfaces, remove rust and strip paint.

➤ **Drill** To drill a straight hole and avoid breaking a bit, hold the drill so that the force you exert helps push the bit straight in. Place the palm of your hand in line with the chuck, extending your index finger along the drill body. Pull the trigger with your second finger.

➤ **Straight in** To drill a hole that's perfectly perpendicular to the surface, tack two scraps of wood together and use the inside corner as a guide.

➤ **How deep?** When drilling to a precise depth, mark the depth on the bit with a piece of masking tape. Cut the piece a little long and stick the overlapping ends together to make a flag. When the right depth is reached, the flag will brush away the debris.

➤ **Bits** A bent bit is likely to break and damage your work. Bits bend easily, so test them for straightness before use. Roll it slowly with your fingertips on a flat surface. If the bit wobbles, it's bent and needs to be discarded.

CAUTION: When drilling, remember that there may be a surprise on the other side. And if you hit something that doesn't feel right, stop.

Twist bit
The standard choice for most holes up to 1/2 in. It bores through wood, dry-wall and metal.

Modified twist bit
It's like the old standard, but with a reengineered tip for faster drilling, easier starting and cleaner holes.

Brad-point bit
The pointed tip lets you position a hole with perfect precision, and the sharp outer edges eliminate wood splintering.

Masonry bit
The carbide tip grinds into concrete, mortar, brick, stucco or stone.

Tile bit
It bores into ceramic tile and even glass. Some versions work with porcelain tile; others don't.

Spade bit
This is the most economical bit for drilling large holes (up to 2 in.) in wood or drywall. Some models have a screw tip for faster drilling.

Wrench or pliers?

➤ **Adjustable wrench** Open the adjustable wrench by turning the screw mechanism. This will open the jaw of the wrench. Make sure it is open a bit more than the size of the nut. Slip the open jaw over the nut and turn the screw mechanism so that it clamps tightly around the nut. Turn in a clockwise direction to tighten it, or counterclockwise to loosen it. Remove the wrench by loosening the screw mechanism. (Never use adjustables where a lot of twisting force is required. They'll break or slip off bolt heads if you apply too much force.)

➤ **Combination wrenches** These wrenches have two different ends—a U-shaped open end and an enclosed "box end." The box end slips over the top of nuts and bolts, the open end slips in from the side.

> **CAUTION:**
> Always turn a nut with a wrench. Using pliers for this purpose will round the edges of the nut and make it even harder to remove later on.

➤ **Socket wrench set** All sets include a wrench handle, an assortment of detachable sockets (sized to fit different nuts and bolts) and a couple of extensions. These snap in place between the wrench handle and sockets, extending the reach of the tool into deeper locations.

➤ **Needle-nose pliers** Needle-nose pliers are finesse tools that let you sneak into confined spaces and grab things that are too small for your fingers or bend wire. They come in both regular and curved-jaw styles.

➤ **Slip-joint pliers** These adjust to two or more positions to accommodate different-size work. Combination jaws grip flat or curved objects. Some models include a crimper.

➤ **Locking pliers** Generically called "vise grips," they come together like a pair of regular pliers as you begin to squeeze them, but they lock shut when closed all the way. They are sold in a huge variety of sizes and jaw styles.

NEEDLE-NOSE PLIERS

➤ **Channel-lock pliers** They use an adjustable jaw design to grip various sizes of round, hexagonal or flat objects. The width of their closed jaws ranges from zero to 4 inches, depending on the size of pliers.

Measure accurately

➤ **Accurate measurements** Use the same measuring tools throughout any project you undertake. Two seemingly identical measuring tools can be off by up to 1/16 in., enough to adversely affect a repair.

➤ **Burn an inch** The hook at the end of a tape measure is designed to slip in and out a little. That movement compensates for the thickness of the hook, depending on whether you're taking inside or outside measurements. But a bent hook or worn rivets can lead to inaccuracy. So when you need precision, bypass hook-related errors by holding the tape at the 1-in. mark and making your mark exactly 1 in. beyond the desired measurement.

➤ **Longer is better** A 20-ft. tape measure is better than a 10-footer, even if you don't need to measure that far. Longer tapes generally have a wider, stiffer blade that will extend farther without bending and falling to the floor. That means you can measure longer distances without a helper holding one end.

➤ **Measure up, not down** When measuring something tall, work with gravity, not against it. To measure ceiling height, for example, butt the tape against the floor and extend it to the ceiling. Bend the tape at the ceiling and "eyeball" the measurement. You'll be able to get within 1/4 in. of the exact height.

➤ **Measure twice for long stretches** When you need to measure a long span and don't have a helper to hold the tape, take two measurements and add them up. This is also a super-accurate way to measure a space that's enclosed on both ends—inside a drawer, for example.

1. Measure halfway to a spot near the center and make a mark exactly at the nearest foot.

2. Measure from the other side and tally up the two measurements.

PENCIL MARK AT 5'

1

THIS MEASUREMENT PLUS 5'

2

> **CAUTION:** A tape measure can hurt you—really. Sounds crazy, but any carpenter will agree: When a tape retracts from several feet out, it can pick up speed and slam into your finger with painful force. Slow it down by holding your finger against the underside of the blade.

Find a stud

➤ **What's a stud?** Studs are simply the vertical 2x4s (or 2x6s) that form the skeleton inside a wall. For heavy-duty projects, you need to know exactly where they are. But for most jobs— like hanging pictures or towel bars—drywall anchors are strong enough.

➤ **Stud spacing** Studs are usually centered 16 in. apart (or sometimes 24 in.). So if you find one, you can find others with only a tape measure.

➤ **Finding studs**

1. **The high-tech way** You can pick up an electronic stud finder at any home center for less than 20 bucks. Just run the gadget horizontally across the wall and it will tell you when it senses a stud. Stud finders work great on drywall. Sometimes they work well on old plaster and lath walls, sometimes not.

1

2. **The detective's way** If you don't have a stud finder handy, or it won't work on your plaster walls, don't give up. The builders of your house left some clues:

a. **Nail holes** Baseboards are almost always nailed to studs. Examine them closely and you'll find tiny dots of wood filler that reveal a stud location.

2a

b. **Switches and outlets** Electrical junction boxes are usually fastened to studs. To determine which side of the box is attached to the stud, you'll have to unscrew the cover plate. Then slip in a business card along the outer side of the box and feel for the stud.

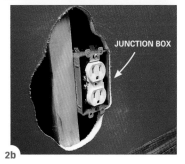

JUNCTION BOX

2b

pro tips!

➤ There's no need to mark up walls with a pencil; a scrap of masking tape will do. If you need pinpoint precision, stick on the tape, then mark with a pencil.

Electrical

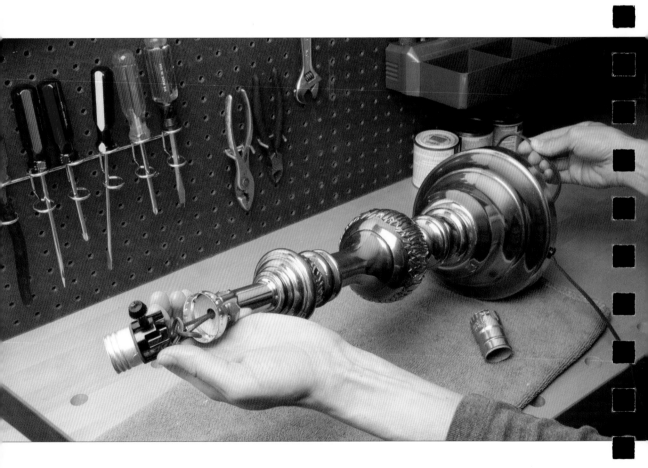

PROFESSIONAL
COST: $45

YOUR COST: $0

SAVINGS: $45

COMPLEXITY
Simple

TOOLS
Voltage tester

Troubleshooting a dead outlet

When an outlet goes dead, it's easy to jump to conclusions and assume the worst. But more often than not, the problem is something simple, and you can save the cost of a service call just by taking a few steps to trace the cause. Don't worry if you're not comfortable doing electrical work. Better than half the time you'll solve the problem without even lifting a tool. We'll show you how to start your search for the problem by checking in the most likely places.

Of course, there will always be problems that are best left to an electrician. But if you take these steps first, there's a good chance you'll find the solution.

Check if other outlets are dead

Take a few minutes to check if other outlets, lights or appliances are affected. Switch lights on and off and test nearby outlets for power (use a voltage tester or plug in a lamp to test the outlets).

Unplug lamps and appliances from dead outlets to eliminate the possibility that a short or overload from one of them is causing the problem. Note the location of dead outlets or mark them with a piece of masking tape so you'll be able to find them again after you've turned off the power.

Check the circuit breakers

After you unplug all the devices from the dead outlets, the next step is to check for a tripped circuit breaker or blown fuse. You'll find the circuit breakers or fuses in the main electrical panel, which is usually located near where the electrical wires enter the house. Garages, basements and laundry rooms are common locations. Locate the panel and open the metal door to reveal the fuses or circuit breakers. Photos 1 – 4 show a typical main panel and the process for resetting a tripped circuit breaker. Remember to turn off your computer before you switch the circuit breakers on and off.

Tripped circuit breakers aren't always apparent. If you don't see a tripped breaker, firmly press every breaker to the "off" position (Photo 3).Then switch them back on. If the tripped breaker won't reset without tripping again, there could be a potentially dangerous short circuit or ground fault condition. Switch the circuit breaker off until you've located the problem. In most cases, a tripped circuit breaker is caused by a temporary overload on the circuit or a short circuit in some device plugged into the circuit. But in rare cases, a loose wire in an electrical box could be causing the problem.

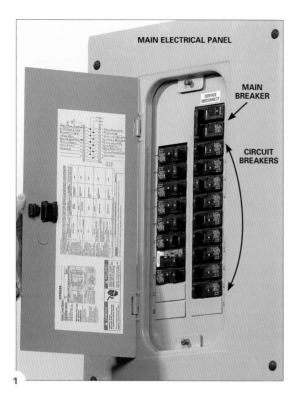

MAIN ELECTRICAL PANEL

SERVICE DISCONNECT

MAIN BREAKER

CIRCUIT BREAKERS

SIEMENS

1. Locate the circuit breaker box (or fuse box) and open the door to search for tripped circuit breakers.

2. Locate tripped breakers by looking for breaker handles that aren't lined up with the rest. Last, push the breaker handles toward the "on" position. Tripped breakers will "give" a little rather than feel solid.

3. The first step in resetting a tripped breaker is to switch it off. Don't just flick the handle; press the handle firmly to the "off" position. You should hear a click.

4. Finally, reset the breaker by pushing the handle firmly to "on." It should line up with all the rest. If it "pops" back to the tripped position, there's a problem in the wiring or in something that's plugged into the circuit.

SWITCH ON

2

TRIPPED CIRCUIT BREAKER

SWITCH OFF

3

SWITCH ON

4

Replace burned-out fuses

1. Look inside the fuse for charred glass or a broken filament—evidence of a blown fuse. Unscrew the suspect fuse and replace it with one of the same type and amperage.

BLOWN FUSE

NON-TAMP-TYPE S

1

Check the GFCIs

GFCI (short for "ground fault circuit interrupter") outlets, those unusual outlets with the test and reset buttons, are required in areas of the house where shock hazards are greatest. They protect against deadly electrical shocks by sensing leaks in the electrical current and immediately tripping to shut off the power. But it's easy to overlook a tripped GFCI as the source of a dead outlet problem. That's because in areas where GFCI-protected outlets are required, electricians often save money by connecting additional standard outlets to one GFCI outlet. A current leak at any one of the outlets will trip the GFCI and cause all of the outlets connected to it to go dead. These GFCI-protected outlets are supposed to be labeled (Photo 1), but the label often falls off.

Look for GFCIs in bathrooms, kitchens, basements, garages and on the home's exterior. Test and reset every GFCI you find (Photo 2). If the GFCI "reset" button doesn't pop out when you press the "test" button, there may be no power to the GFCI or you may have a bad GFCI. On the other hand, if the "reset" button trips again every time you press it, there may be a dangerous current leak somewhere on the circuit. In either case, solving the problem requires additional electrical testing that we won't cover here. Refer to other electrical repair manuals or call an electrician for help.

1. **Identification label.** Protected "downstream" receptacle should be labeled if they have GFCI protection.

2. **Push reset button.** You can test GFCI receptacles by pushing the "test" button and then the "reset" button.

STICKER ON A STANDARD OUTLET THAT IS CONNECTED TO A GFCI

1

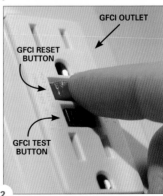

GFCI OUTLET

GFCI RESET BUTTON

GFCI TEST BUTTON

2

Install an in-line cord switch

Add an in-line switch so you don't have to reach under the lampshade to flip on a light. The installation is fast, simple and doesn't require any special tools.

Mount an in-line switch on the cord. Several sizes of in-line cord switches are available at hardware stores, home centers and lamp specialty stores. Look at the tiny printing on the cord to determine which size switch you need, SPT-1 or SPT-2. Consult the instruction sheet before installation.

Note: Connect an in-line switch only to a cord with a polarized plug. A polarized plug has one prong wider than the other so you can only insert it one way into an outlet.

1. Unplug lamp. Slit the cord where you want the switch. Use a small pocketknife to make a 3/4-in. slit at the desired switch location. Do not cut into the individual wire sheathing.

2. Cut apart the smooth, non-identified (hot) wire at the center of the split.

3. Attach the switch. Insert the cord into the wire channel on the switch bottom. Press the switch halves together and tighten the switch screw.

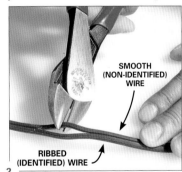

|← 3/4" →|

1

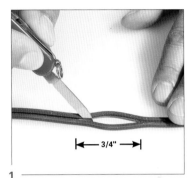

SMOOTH (NON-IDENTIFIED) WIRE

RIBBED (IDENTIFIED) WIRE

2

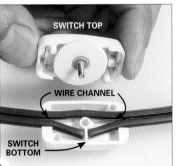

SWITCH TOP

WIRE CHANNEL

SWITCH BOTTOM

3

PROFESSIONAL COST: $105

YOUR COST: $15

SAVINGS: $90

COMPLEXITY
Simple

TOOLS
4-in-1 screwdriver
Wire stripper/cutter
Pocketknife or utility knife

MATERIALS
In-line cord switch

PROFESSIONAL
COST: $90

YOUR COST: $0

SAVINGS: $90

COMPLEXITY
Simple

TOOLS
Straight-slot
screwdriver

MATERIALS
Bulb

Fix a flickering lamp

Fix a flickering lamp light bulb in several easy steps. First, try tightening the bulb in the socket and plugging the lamp into a different outlet. If the lamp still flickers, unplug it and check the cord for fraying where it enters the plug. Replace it if necessary. If the cord's in good shape, chances are the bulb isn't fully contacting the metal contact tab located at the bottom of the lamp socket. Make sure the lamp is unplugged, and adjust the contact tab as shown in the photo below.

Replace the bulb and turn on the lamp. If the problem persists, the lamp switch, socket or cord is worn out.

1. Unplug the lamp, unscrew the bulb and gently pry the metal contact tab 1/8 in. up off the bottom of the lamp socket with a straight-slot screwdriver. Scrape off rust or corrosion with the screwdriver and blow any grit out of the socket.

CONTACT TAB

LAMP SOCKET

1

CAUTION:
Unplug lamp before beginning repair.

Replace a problem plug

Plugs on lamp cords often have a weak point where the cord enters the plug. Pulling and flexing can break the wires at this point, leaving you with a lamp that flickers when you jiggle the cord. The cure is to replace the plug. To do this safely, choose a polarized plug. A polarized plug has one blade that's wider than the other so it fits into an outlet only one way. Before you buy a plug, take a close look at the cord. Along with other labeling, you should find "SPT-1" or "SPT-2." This refers to the thickness of the cord's sheathing, and the plug you buy must have the same listing so it will fit over the sheathing.

   The plug you buy may not look exactly like the one shown here, but installing it will be similar. Be sure to read the manufacturer's instructions.

PROFESSIONAL COST: $90

YOUR COST: $5

SAVINGS: $85

COMPLEXITY
Simple

TOOLS
Pocketknife or utility knife
4-in-1 screwdriver

MATERIALS
Polarized replacement plug

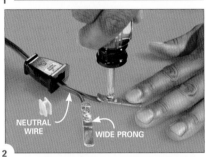

1. Cut the cord a couple of inches from the plug. Then split about an inch of cord with a pocketknife and strip off 3/4 in. of insulation. Do not expose any wire. If you do, cut back the cord and start over.

2. Wrap the wires clockwise around the terminal screws of the new plug and tighten. The neutral wire must connect to the wider prong.

NEUTRAL WIRE   WIDE PRONG

3. Slip the blades into the housing and push the blade holder into place.

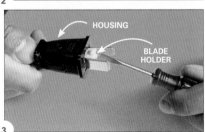

HOUSING

BLADE HOLDER

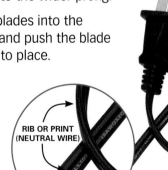

WIDE BLADE (NEUTRAL WIRE)

RIB OR PRINT (NEUTRAL WIRE)

The neutral wire connects to the wide plug blade and is distinguished from the hot wire by ribs, color, printing or indentations in the plastic insulation.

Replace a lamp socket

A lamp socket itself can go bad, but more often it's the switch inside the socket. Either way, the solution is replacement. Regardless of the existing switch type, you can choose a push-through switch, a pull chain, a turn knob or a three-way turn knob that provides two brightness levels. You can also choose a socket without a switch and install a switch cord instead.

CAUTION:
Pull the plug before working on a lamp.

1. Pry the socket shell out of its base with a screwdriver. Cut the wires to remove the socket. Then loosen the setscrew so you can unscrew the socket base.

2. Unscrew the socket base from the threaded tube. If the base won't spin off by hand, grab the tube and the base with a pliers to spin it free. Then screw on the new base and tighten the setscrew.

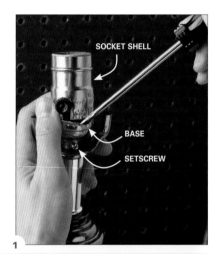

1

pro tips!

➤ An underwriter's knot prevents the wires from pulling out of the screw terminals when the cord is tugged. **Note:** Black and white wires used for photo clarity.

2

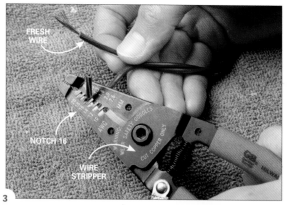

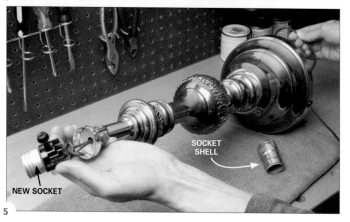

3. Strip off 1/2 in. of insulation with a wire stripper (start with notches labeled 16) and twist the wire strands together. If you pull off any wire strands while stripping, cut back the cord and start over using larger notches.

4. Tie an underwriter's knot in the cord. Then connect the wires by wrapping them clockwise around the screws and tightening. Connect the neutral wire to the silver screw.

   To identify the neutral wire, start at the plug. The wider plug blade is connected to the neutral wire, and you'll find that the neutral wire is distinguished from the "hot" wire by different colors, printing, or tiny ribs/indentations in the plastic insulation. If your old plug blades are of equal width, replace the plug and cord along with the socket.

5. Pull the excess cord down through the lamp. Slip the insulation sleeve and socket shell over the socket and snap the shell into the base.

PROFESSIONAL
COST: $90

YOUR COST: $20

SAVINGS: $70

COMPLEXITY
Simple

TOOLS
4-in-1 screwdriver
Voltage tester

MATERIALS
Pull-chain fixture

Replace a pull-chain light fixture

Pull-chain light fixtures are easy to replace when the switch wears out or breaks. We show you how to replace it safely and quickly. It'll only take about 15 minutes.

Pull-chain fixtures are made from either plastic or porcelain, but we recommend the porcelain because it withstands heat better and lasts longer.

Caution: Before starting, flip the circuit breaker off or pull the fuse to disconnect the power to the light, then test to make sure the power is off (Photo 1). There may be an unused bare ground wire inside the electrical box (Photo 3). If it falls down while you're replacing the fixture, wrap it in a circle and push it up as far into the electrical box as possible.

....

> **CAUTION:**
> Turn off power at the main panel.

1. **Test for hot wires.**
   Turn off the power, remove the light bulb and unscrew the fixture from the electrical box. Pull the fixture down, but keep your hands away from the wires. Touch one voltage tester probe to the black wire, and the other to the white wire. If the voltage indicator doesn't light up, the power is off.

1

TERMINAL SCREWS

BROKEN PULL SWITCH

2

2. **Disconnect the wires.** Loosen the terminal screws and unhook the wiring from the old fixture. If the wire ends are broken or corroded, strip off 3/4 in. of sheathing and bend the bare wire end into a hook.

3. **Connect the new fixture.** Attach the black wire to the gold terminal screw on the new fixture and the white wire to the silver terminal screw. Wrap the wires clockwise so they cover at least three-quarters of the terminal screws. Firmly tighten the screws so the copper wire compresses slightly. Twist the fixture to spiral the wires into the electrical box. Screw the new fixture to the box snugly, but don't overtighten it or the porcelain might crack.

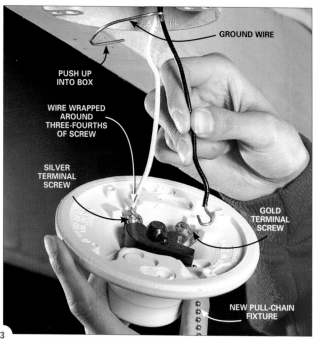

GROUND WIRE

PUSH UP INTO BOX

WIRE WRAPPED AROUND THREE-FOURTHS OF SCREW

SILVER TERMINAL SCREW

GOLD TERMINAL SCREW

NEW PULL-CHAIN FIXTURE

3

PROFESSIONAL
COST: $75

YOUR COST: $15

SAVINGS: $60

COMPLEXITY
Simple

TOOLS
4-in-1 screwdriver
Wire stripper/cutter

MATERIALS
Replacement bulb
Fluorescent socket

> **CAUTION:**
> Turn off the circuit
> at the main panel.

Replace a fluorescent light bulb and socket

Fluorescent light bulbs typically last many years, but when one flickers on and off, or the end turns light gray to black in color, it needs to be replaced. Another common problem is cracked sockets, caused by bumps from other objects or stress from removing a bulb.

1. Unplug the light and twist the bulb 90 degrees with both hands. Pull one end straight down to free it from the socket and then lower the entire bulb. Replace the bulb with the same size bulb.

2. Shut down the power and remove the bulb(s). Unscrew the fixture end cover. Screw locations will vary, but double-bulb units typically have a screw on each side, and four-bulb units typically have an additional screw on the top center edge. Remove all screws and pull off the cover.

BAD BULB
DISCOLORED
END

LIGHT
UNPLUGGED

1

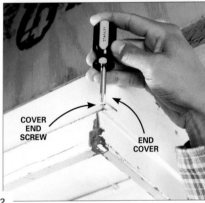

COVER
END
SCREW

END
COVER

2

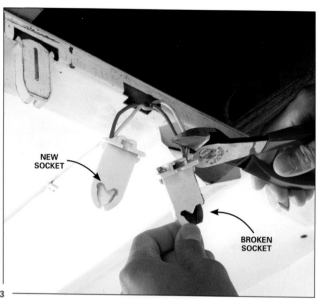

NEW SOCKET

BROKEN SOCKET

3

3. Slide out the socket to expose the wiring. There will be two or four wires coming into the socket. It's very important to keep the wiring order straight, so cut one side of the old socket wiring loose at a time. Strip the wiring back 1/2 in.

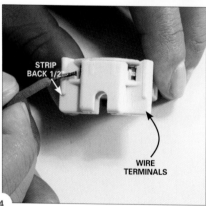

STRIP BACK 1/2"

WIRE TERMINALS

4

4. Press the bare wire ends into the terminal slots on the new socket, being careful to insert the correct wire into each terminal. The terminal slot works like a barbed fish hook; once a wire is pushed in, it cannot be pulled out. Repeat the process for the remaining wires and then replace the socket.

Note: If the fixture still doesn't work, then the ballast is probably shot and it's time to buy a new fixture.

pro tips!

➤ The ballast boosts the incoming voltage to start the tubes and then regulates the current to provide continuous light. Ballast replacement can cost as much as a new fixture, so buying a new fixture may be a better investment.

How to balance a ceiling fan

PROFESSIONAL
COST: $85

YOUR COST: $0

SAVINGS: $85

COMPLEXITY
Simple

TOOLS
Yardstick

MATERIALS
Fan blade
  balancing kit

If your ceiling fan wobbles and makes more racket than an unbalanced washing machine load, read on; we've got the fix for you. Ceiling fan wobble is caused by imbalances in the fan blades or blade holders, misalignment of blades, excess dust accumulation or just loose blade holder mounting screws. Restore your fan to its smooth-running days of old before you wear down the moving parts.

First, make sure all the blades are tightly screwed into the blade holder, and the blade holder is firmly screwed into the fan flywheel. Remove any dust or buildup from the fan blades with a household cleaner. Run the fan to check the wobble and to dry the fan blades. If the wobble persists, one of the blades may be out of alignment.

1. Make sure the blades are straight. Measure the distance from the ceiling to the edge of a blade with a yardstick (most blades are angled, so be sure to measure on the same side of all the blades). Hold the yardstick still and rotate the blades around to measure the other blades.

   If any blade is out of alignment, gently bend the blade holder up or down until the blade is in line with the others.

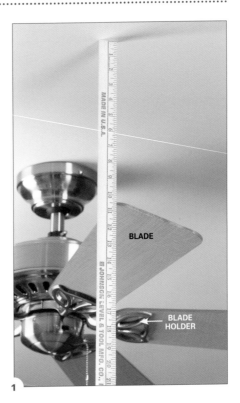

BLADE

BLADE HOLDER

1

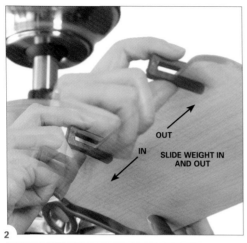

OUT

IN   SLIDE WEIGHT IN AND OUT

2

ADHESIVE-BACKED WEIGHT

3

2. Turn the fan on to see if it spins smoothly. If it still wobbles, pick up a blade balancing kit from a hardware store or home center. The balancing clip will balance the fan blades, eliminating the wobble.

   Slide the balancing clip on the trailing edge of any blade, halfway between the holder and tip. Run the fan to check the wobble. Repeat with each blade, noting which one most reduced the wobble, then slide the clip in small increments away from the center of that blade. Move the clip, operate the fan, then move it again until you eliminate as much wobble as possible.

3. Set a weight. Peel off the backing and stick the adhesive-backed balancing weight on the top center of the blade directly in line with the balancing clip. Add more weight if needed to get a smooth-running fan.

BALANCING CLIP

ADHESIVE-BACKED WEIGHTS

5GM

5M

3GM

3GM

THE BALANCING KIT CONTAINS THE BLADE CLIP PLUS SEVERAL ADHESIVE-BACKED WEIGHTS.

PROFESSIONAL
COST: $200

YOUR COST: $40

SAVINGS: $160

COMPLEXITY
Simple

TOOLS
Cordless drill
4-in-1 screwdriver
Level
Drill bit set

MATERIALS
Clothespin
Tape
Wall anchors

CAUTION:
If your old
thermostat contains
mercury, you'll see
a small glass tube
with a shiny silver
ball inside. Mercury
is toxic. Take this
type of thermostat
to a hazardous
waste disposal site.

How to install a programmable thermostat

Save a lot of money! Learn how to remove your old thermostat and install a new programmable thermostat—with no rewiring required.

You can reduce your home's heating and cooling costs by about 15 percent with a programmable thermostat. It automatically keeps the temperature at a comfortable level when you're home, but switches to an energy-saving level when you're away or asleep. Programmable thermostats are available from home centers and hardware stores. The higher-priced models provide more programming options.

1. Turn off power to the heating and cooling systems at the main panel. Remove the old thermostat. There will be anywhere from two to five wires hooked up to the old thermostat. Mark the wires with a tab (or tape) and the letter that represents the terminal and unscrew them. Remove and discard the old thermostat.

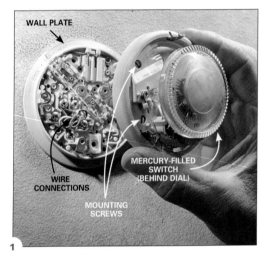

WALL PLATE

MERCURY-FILLED
SWITCH
(BEHIND DIAL)

WIRE
CONNECTIONS

MOUNTING
SCREWS

1

CAUTION:
Programmable thermostats will work with most gas or oil furnaces and central air conditioners. However, heat pumps, electric baseboards and a few other systems require special features. Read the package to make sure the programmable thermostat you buy is compatible with your heating and cooling system. If you're unsure, call your local utility or a heating and cooling contractor.

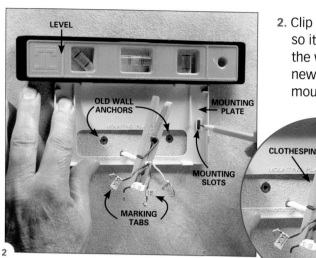

2

2. Clip a clothespin to the cable so it doesn't slide down inside the wall cavity and mount the new wall plate. Level the new mounting plate in position and mark the mounting screw holes. Drill 3/16-in. holes, insert drywall anchors and screw the plate to the wall.

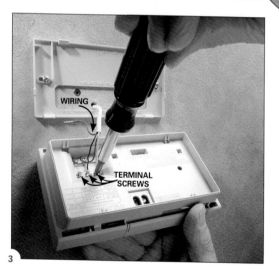

3

3. If the thermostat has back-up batteries, insert them before wiring the new thermostat. Screw the system wiring to the screw terminals on the new thermostat using the letter labels as reference (strip the wires back if necessary). These letters are standard; hook them up to the same terminals on the new thermostat. Snap the thermostat to the mounting plate.

pro tips!

➤ The thermostat may need to be configured to your heating system. It may also come preprogrammed, but to maximize savings, set it up according to your schedule. Consult the instructions that come with the thermostat for system adjustments and programming. You won't save energy if the thermostat isn't programmed correctly.

PROFESSIONAL
COST: $110

YOUR COST: $20

SAVINGS: $90

COMPLEXITY
Moderate

TOOLS
Tape measure
4-in-1 screwdriver
Needle-nose pliers
Non-contact voltage
 detector
Voltage tester,
 2 lead wire type
Wire stripper/cutter

MATERIALS
Dimmer switch
Wire connectors

> **CAUTION:**
> Call an electrician if
> the original switch
> is connected to
> two white wires.
> This may indicate
> a dangerous
> switched neutral.

How to install a dimmer switch

It doesn't take long to replace an ordinary light switch with a full-feature dimmer. But while you're at it, to make your home safer, you should upgrade the wiring to meet the latest requirements of the National Electrical Code.

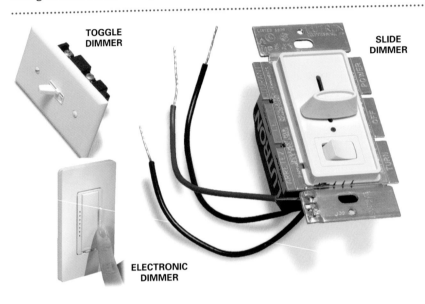

TOGGLE DIMMER

SLIDE DIMMER

ELECTRONIC DIMMER

Buying dimmers

If the switch you're replacing is the only switch controlling the light, buy a standard single-pole dimmer. If the light can be switched on and off from two or more switches, buy a three-way dimmer switch. But you won't be able to dim the lights from every switch location unless you buy a set of special dimmers with advanced electronics and install one at each switch location.

Most dimmers are designed to handle 600 watts. Add up the wattage of all the light bulbs you'll be dimming. Then read the dimmer package to make sure it can handle the load. Heavy-duty 1,000- and 1,500-watt dimmers are also readily available. Read the package if you'll be installing dimmers side by side in the same electrical box because the wattage rating is reduced to compensate for extra heat buildup.

Finally, you have to use a special device, not a dimmer, to control the speed of ceiling fans and motors. Most fluorescent lights can't be dimmed without altering the fixture.

> **CAUTION:** If you have aluminum wiring, don't work on it yourself. The connections require special techniques. Call in a licensed pro who's certified to work with it. This wiring is dull gray, not the dull orange that's characteristic of copper.

1. **Check for hot wires.** Turn off the power at the main circuit panel. Hold the tip of a non-contact voltage detector near each screw terminal to be sure the power is off. Then unscrew the switch and pull it from the box. Probe around inside the box with the detector to make sure there are no other hot wires from another circuit.

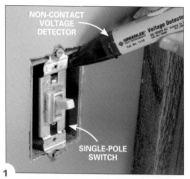

pro tips!

➤ Non-contact voltage detectors are available at hardware stores and home centers. This type of tester is prefered because it detects voltage without direct contact with the metal conductor. That's huge—it means you can check potentially hot wires before you handle them.

2. **Calculate box volume.** Measure the height, width and depth of metal boxes and refer to the chart below to determine the box volume. Plastic boxes have their volume stamped inside.

Make sure the box is large enough

Too many wires and devices stuffed into a box can cause dangerous overheating, short-circuiting and fires. The National Electrical Code specifies minimum box sizes to reduce this risk.

To figure the minimum box size required by the electrical code, add 1 for each hot and neutral wire entering the box, 1 for all the ground wires combined, 1 for all the clamps combined, and 2 for each device (switch or receptacle) installed in the box. Multiply this figure by 2 for 14-gauge wire and 2.25 for 12-gauge wire to get the minimum box volume in cubic inches.

To help determine the gauge of the wire in your switch box, look at the amperage of the circuit breaker or fuse in the main electrical panel. Fifteen-amp circuits are usually wired with 14-gauge wire and 20-amp circuits require 12-gauge or heavier wire.

Compare the figure you get with the volume of your existing box. Plastic boxes have the volume stamped inside, usually on the back. Steel box capacities are listed in the electrical code. We've

FIGURE A	
Height/width/depth (inches)	Volume (cubic inches)
3 x 2 x 2-1/4	10.5
3 x 2 x 2-1/2	12.5
3 x 2 x 2-3/4	14.0

listed the volume of the most common steel boxes in Figure A. If you have a steel box, measure it (Photo 2) and consult the chart to see if it's large enough. If your box is too small, replace it with a larger one. It's possible to replace a box without cutting away the wall, but it's a tricky job. It's easier to remove about a 16-in. square of drywall or plaster and patch it after the new large box is installed.

pro tips!

➤ If the circuit breaker is labeled "15 amp," the wires are probably 14-gauge, or 12-gauge for 20-amp circuit breakers.

Test your ground before you connect it

New dimmers have either a green grounding wire or a green ground screw that you'll have to connect to a grounding source if one is available. Houses wired with plastic-sheathed cable almost always have bare copper ground wires that you'll connect to the dimmer. But test first using the procedure shown in Photo 3 to verify that the wire is connected to a ground.

Some wiring systems, like ours, rely on metal conduit for the ground. If you have one of these systems, Photo 3 shows how to test the metal box

to verify that it's grounded. If it is, attach a short ground wire to the metal box with either a metal grounding clip as shown in Photos 4 and 5 or a green grounding screw screwed into the threaded hole in the back of the box. Then connect it to the dimmer.

If testing reveals your box isn't grounded, you can still install the dimmer, but you must use a plastic cover plate and make sure no bare metal parts are exposed.

3. **Test for ground**. Turn the power back on. Then place the leads of a voltage tester between each screw terminal and the metal box. If the tester lights, the box is grounded. **Caution: Turn off the power again before proceeding.**

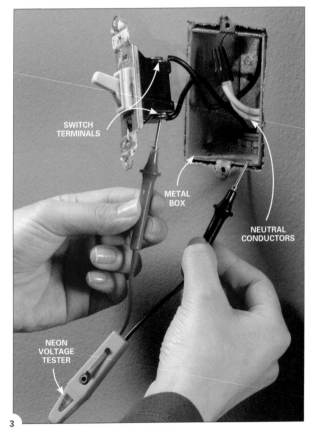

SWITCH TERMINALS

METAL BOX

NEUTRAL CONDUCTORS

NEON VOLTAGE TESTER

3

4. **Install a grounding clip.** Press a grounding clip and 6-in. length of bare copper wire onto the metal box with a screwdriver. Cut away a little bit of drywall under the box to provide clearance for the clip.

5. **Pinch the wire end.** Bend the ground wire back onto the clip and squeeze it down tight so it won't interfere with the dimmer switch.

6. **Strip new wire ends.** Clip off the bent end of each wire with the wire cutter. Strip 3/8 in. of insulation from the end of the wires.

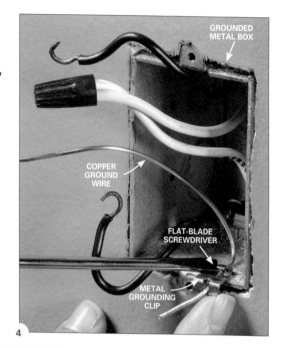

GROUNDED METAL BOX

COPPER GROUND WIRE

FLAT-BLADE SCREWDRIVER

METAL GROUNDING CLIP

4

BEND AND PINCH WIRE

NEEDLE-NOSE PLIERS

NOTCH OUT DRYWALL

5

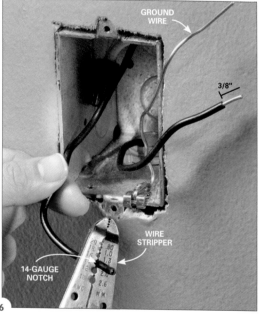

GROUND WIRE

3/8"

WIRE STRIPPER

14-GAUGE NOTCH

6

The easy part is installing the dimmer

Some dimmers, like the one we're installing, have stranded wires attached. Photos 7 and 8 show how to install this type of dimmer. Others have screw terminals instead. For these, strip 3/4 in. of the insulated covering from the wires in the box and bend a loop in each with a needle-nose pliers. Place the loop clockwise around the screw terminals and close the loop around the screws with the needle-nose pliers. Then tighten the screws.

It doesn't matter if you reverse the two switch wires to a single-pole dimmer. But if you're replacing a three-way switch with a three-way dimmer, label the "common" wire (it'll be labeled on the old switch) when you remove the old switch so you can connect it to the "common" terminal on the dimmer.

In most cases, the two switch wires will be some color other than green or white, usually black. But one of the wires may be white if your house is wired with plastic-sheathed cable (like Romex). Put a wrap of black tape around the white conductor to label it as a hot wire.

7. **Connect the wires.** Hold the wires together with the stranded wire protruding about 1/8 in. beyond the solid wire. Match the size of the wire connector you're using to the size and number of wires being connected. Check the manufacturer's specifications on the package to be sure. Twist a plastic wire connector clockwise onto the wires to connect them. Stop twisting when the connector is snug.

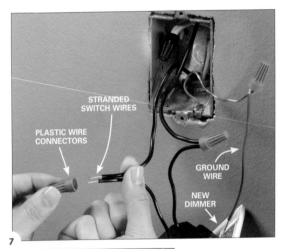

STRANDED SWITCH WIRES

PLASTIC WIRE CONNECTORS

GROUND WIRE

NEW DIMMER

7

8. **Attach the cover plate.** Fold the wires neatly into the box. Screw the dimmer to the box with the screws provided. Finish the job by installing the cover plate and turning on the power to test the new dimmer.

NEW DIMMER SWITCH

SCREW TO BOX

8

Replace a phone jack

A dead line or static on your phone may be due to a bad wall jack. Replace it in 10 minutes.

PROFESSIONAL COST: $85

YOUR COST: $10

SAVINGS: $75

COMPLEXITY
Simple

TOOLS
4-in-1 screwdriver
Needle-nose pliers

MATERIALS
New wall jack

1. Remove the two screws on the jack faceplate and disconnect the old jack. Loosen the terminal screws on the back of the jack and disconnect the wiring. Hold on to the wire when you remove the jack so it doesn't slide out the back of the box. If the ends of the wires are free of corrosion, you can reuse them, but if not, cut them back (leave enough wire to work with) and strip off 1/2 in. of sheathing.

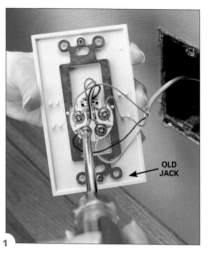

OLD JACK

2. Connect the new jack. Pinch the wire sheathing against the back of the new jack with your thumb. Hold the tip of the bare wire with a needle-nose pliers, and wrap it clockwise around the terminal. If the wires from the wall and the jack are the same color combination, simply match them up. If they don't match, see the chart. Before you mount the new jack to the wall, make sure the bare wires don't touch each other.

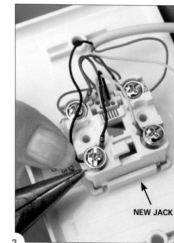

NEW JACK

Std. Cable	Corresponding colors in other cables	
Red	Blue	Blue/White dashes
Green	Blue/White	White/Blue dashes
Yellow	Orange	Orange/White dashes
Black	Orange/White	White/Orange dashes

Repair the TV remote

PROFESSIONAL
COST: $100

YOUR COST: $30

SAVINGS: $70

COMPLEXITY
Simple

TOOLS
Small screwdriver
Butter knife
Digital camera

MATERIALS
Old toothbrush
Repair kit
Dishwashing liquid

Most of the time you can fix your TV remote yourself with a simple repair kit and avoid the high cost of a replacement.

Most remotes have electrically conductive paint on the bottom of each rubber button. The more you use each button, the more the paint wears off. The good news: You can buy a repair kit that includes two-part conductive paint. (We used the Chemtronics CW2605 rubber keypad repair kit, at mcmelectronics.com.) The bad news: You have to figure out how to disassemble the remote, and each one is different. But here are some general disassembly tips.

1. Start by removing the screws. They're usually hidden in the battery compartment under labels and rubber feet. Next, take a digital photo of the remote with the screws near their holes. Be sure you get a clear shot of all the buttons and any slide switches along the side of the remote. Once you pop open the remote, those slide switches may fly out.

To separate the halves, press a butter knife along the seam and look for "give." Press in at those points and pry the halves apart. Inside you'll find either individual rubber buttons or a single molded sheet containing all the buttons. If you've spilled anything sticky on your remote, dunk the rubber buttons/sheet, plastic case and any hard plastic buttons in a bowl of warm water and dishwashing liquid. Brush off the debris, rinse all the parts with warm water and let them dry.

DISHWASHING LIQUID
AND WATER

CIRCUIT
BOARD

1

2. Follow the mixing and application instructions. Repaint each button with a new coat of conductive paint. (Paint all of them as long as you have the case open.) The paint dries in about 24 hours, but it needs a full 72 hours to cure completely. That's why we had you take digital photos—so you could remember how to reassemble your remote three days later. Don't rush the curing process or you'll be repeating the repair in a year or so. Reassemble the remote and you're ready to surf.

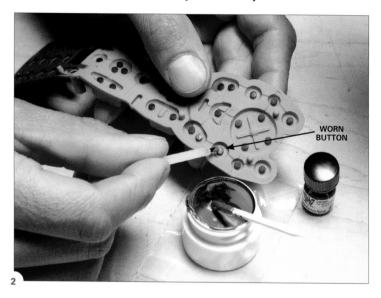

WORN BUTTON

2

Chapter 3
Plumbing

Shut off the main water valve

YOUR COST: $0

SAVINGS: $60

COMPLEXITY
Simple

TOOLS
Wrench
Hammer

MATERIALS
Lubricant or
penetrating oil
if required

Your main shutoff valve is one of the most important disaster-stoppers in your home. When a pipe leaks or bursts, this valve lets you shut off water flow to your entire home. Take a few minutes to locate and test to make sure you can close it. In most cases, you'll find two valves—one before the water meter and one after. Closing either of them will do the trick. If you have a well, shut off the electrical switch for the well when you leave for an extended period so it won't pump any water while you're gone.

There are two types of main shutoff valves:

Ball valve The stainless steel ball almost always rotates smoothly to shut off the water. But just to be sure, give the handle a quarter-turn. Then turn on a faucet to see if the water is off.

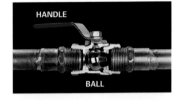

Gate valves Most common in older homes. The valve closes when a wedge-shaped brass gate is lowered into a slot.

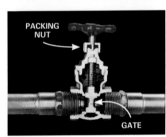

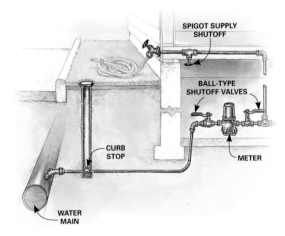

Indoor shutoff In colder climates, the main water shutoff is typically in the basement.

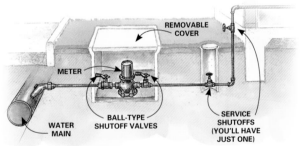

Outdoor shutoff In warmer climates, the main water shutoff is typically outside, attached to an exterior wall or in an accessible underground box.

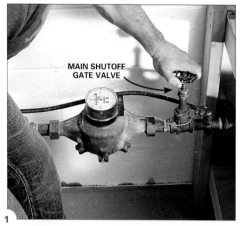

1. MAIN SHUTOFF GATE VALVE

1. A gate valve is prone to getting stuck open, closed or somewhere in between—especially after years without use.

2. STEM   PACKING NUT

2. To close a gate valve, turn the handle clockwise. If you can't turn the handle, loosen the packing nut just a little. But be sure to hold the handle in position while you turn the nut. If the handle turns as you unscrew the nut, you risk breaking the valve. A shot of lubricant or penetrating oil may also help. Then try again.

3.

3. Reopening a stubborn gate valve is more risky than closing it; you're more likely to break internal parts and could end up without running water. If the valve is stuck closed, tap it with a hammer gently (Photo 3). When the valve opens a little, stop for a few minutes. That allows water pressure on both sides of the valve to equalize, instead of pressing against one side and locking the valve in place.

CAUTION:
Shut off the water supply to your entire home when you leave for overnight or longer.
   Every insurance adjuster has a hundred stories like this one: The homeowners left town Friday and returned Sunday to find thousands of dollars in water damage. The moral of the story: Before going on vacation, turn off the main valve. In less than a minute, you can eliminate the most common cause of home damage.

COMPLEXITY
Simple

TOOLS
Wrench set or
 basin wrench

MATERIALS
New sink sprayer
 and hose

Replace a sink sprayer and hose

Replace a leaky or clogged sprayer hose and head in 15 minutes. The trick is getting to the hose connection under the sink.

Over time, sink sprayers often break or become clogged with mineral deposits. Or the sprayer hose can harden and crack or wear through from rubbing against something under the sink. The best solution in these cases is replacement. You can pick up just the sprayer head or a head and hose kit at a home center or hardware store.

Photo 1 shows how to remove the entire sprayer head and hose assembly. You may be able to get a small open-end wrench up to the sprayer hose nipple, but space is very tight. If there isn't enough room to turn the wrench, you'll have to purchase a basin wrench at a home center or hardware store.

1. Use an open-end or basin wrench to unscrew the sprayer hose from the hose nipple. Pull the old sprayer and hose out of the sink grommet. Slide the new hose through the grommet on top of the sink and reconnect it to the faucet.

2. Hold the base of the sprayer in your hand and twist off the sprayer head. Screw on the new head.

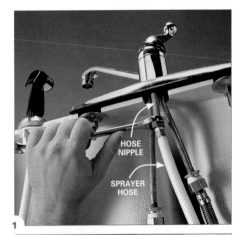

HOSE NIPPLE

SPRAYER HOSE

1

SPRAYER HEAD

SINK GROMMET

2

How to fix a chipped sink

You can fix chipped enamel on cast iron and steel sinks and you can make the repair almost invisible with a special enamel repair kit. We show you how.

You can find two-component epoxy (catalyst and hardener) in the adhesive section of most hardware stores and home centers. It's usually available in a variety of colors. If necessary, two colors can be mixed for a more precise match.

PROFESSIONAL COST: $400

YOUR COST: $10

SAVINGS: $390

COMPLEXITY
Simple

MATERIALS
Sponge
Wet/dry sandpaper, 400- or 600-grit
Epoxy repair kit
Small brush

1. First, scrub the chipped area thoroughly with a sponge and soapy water. Then rub 400- to 600-grit "wet-and-dry" sandpaper over the damaged area to remove dirt and rust, as well as rough up the chip so epoxy will stick to it.

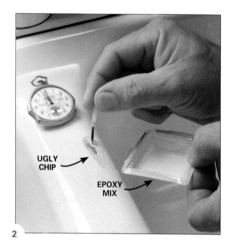

UGLY CHIP

EPOXY MIX

2

2. Mix the two epoxy ingredients according to label directions. Match the enamel color and dab it into the chipped area to fill the hole. Use a small brush to fill the chip. If the chip is deep, apply the material in several coats, and don't forget to allow for the drying time specified on the label. Once the repair is complete, wait 24 hours before you use the sink, and don't scrub that area for seven days.

COMPLEXITY
Simple

TOOLS
Slip-joint pliers
Small screwdriver or
knife

MATERIALS
Electrical tape
Toothbrush

Restore free flow to a clogged aerator

If the flow from your kitchen or bathroom faucet isn't what it used to be, the aerator is probably plugged. An aerator can clog slowly as mineral deposits build up, or quickly after plumbing work loosens debris inside pipes. Usually, a quick cleaning solves the problem.

1. Wrap the jaws of a pliers with electrical tape and unscrew the aerator. Close the stopper so the small parts can't fall down the drain.

2. Disassemble the aerator and lay out the parts in the order you remove them to make reassembly foolproof. You may need a small screwdriver or knife to pry the components apart. Scrub the parts and reassemble them. Gunk can also build up inside the faucet neck, so clean it out with your finger and flush out the loosened debris.

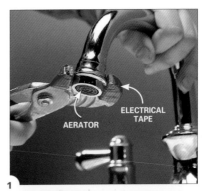

AERATOR   ELECTRICAL TAPE

1

2

pro tips!

➤ If the mineral buildup resists scrubbing and you have a standard cylinder-shaped aerator, you can replace it. Take your old aerator along to the home center or hardware store to find a match. If your aerator has a fancy shape (like the one shown here), finding a match won't be as simple. So try this first: Soak the aerator parts in vinegar overnight to soften mineral buildup. If that doesn't work, search online for the brand of your faucet followed by "faucet parts." With a little searching, you can find diagrams of your faucet and order a new aerator.

Unclog a bathroom sink without chemicals

Slow-moving or stopped-up drains are common in bathroom sinks, but luckily the fix is usually simple and takes only about 15 minutes. The problem is caused by hair and gummy soap scum that get caught on the stopper or pivot rod and clog the drain.

PROFESSIONAL
COST: $100

YOUR COST: $0

SAVINGS: $100

COMPLEXITY
Simple

TOOLS
Slip-joint pliers

MATERIALS
Stiff wire or
 wire coat hanger

1. Tug gently on the stopper to see if it'll come out. If so, remove it. Sometimes it'll come right out. If it doesn't lift out, it's held in by the pivot rod.

2. Unscrew the pivot rod nut and pull out the rod. (If you can't loosen the nut by hand, use pliers.) With the pivot rod pulled out, you'll be able to lift out the stopper.

3. To get the clog out, bend a wire in a tight hook (a light-duty clothes hanger or short length of electrical wire will do) and fish out the hair. Run hot water down the drain to help clear out any remaining soap scum and to check that the clog is gone.

   If you didn't have to remove the pivot rod to remove the stopper, you can just drop the stopper back down into the drain. If you removed the pivot rod, first drop the stopper into the drain. Then line up the pivot rod with the slot in the stopper and reinsert it. Finally, hand-tighten the pivot rod nut. Check around the pivot rod nut to make sure it's not leaking. If you see drips, tighten the pivot rod nut slightly with pliers.

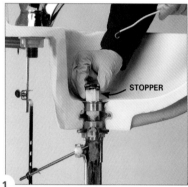

STOPPER

1

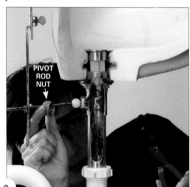

PIVOT
ROD
NUT

2

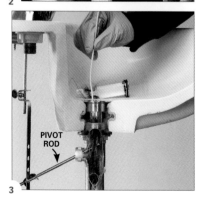

PIVOT
ROD

3

Quickly fix leaky cartridge-type faucets

We'll take the mystery out of cartridge-type faucets and show you how to fix them yourself. Regardless of where the faucet is leaking, you can make the DIY repair by following the steps below. It doesn't take any plumbing expertise, and it'll finally put an end to that annoying leak.

If your faucet leaks from the spout, replace the seats and springs (Photos 1 – 3). If it continues to drip from the spout after replacing the seats and springs, replace the cartridge, too. If your faucet leaks around the handles, the O-rings on the cartridge are bad. Buy a new kit that includes a new cartridge and O-rings.

1. Shut off the water to the sink. Remove the faucet handles. Most are held on by retaining screws under the caps on the top of the handles. (Our handles were held on with small Allen screws located under the handle.) Then unscrew the large nut that holds the cartridge in.

10" ADJUSTABLE WRENCH

CARTRIDGE RETAINING NUT

1

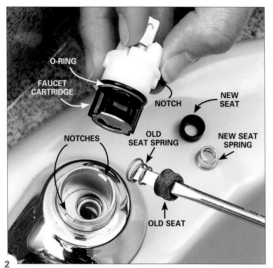

2. Pull straight up on the cartridge to remove it. Use pliers if you have to, but be sure to protect the cartridge with tape or a rag. Note the orientation of the cartridge to the notches in the faucet so you can reinstall it the same way. Remove the old seat and spring with a small screwdriver.

3. Drop the new spring into the recess and push the new seat in with your finger. Spread a thin layer of plumber's grease around the cartridge. Push the cartridge into the faucet, aligning it with the notches. Then tighten the large retaining nut with the wrench and replace the handles.

Leaks usually develop on the hot side, but replace the seats on both hot and cold sides while you're at it.

pro tips!

➤ New faucets are easy to take apart and replacement parts are readily available at most hardware stores, home centers and plumbing supply stores. Of course, there are still many different brands and styles, so it's best to shut the water off, disassemble the faucet and take the parts along to assure a perfect match.

PROFESSIONAL
COST: $150

YOUR COST: $0

SAVINGS: $150

COMPLEXITY
Simple

TOOLS
Screwdriver
Wrench
Seat wrench

MATERIALS
Washers
Valve seat
Heat-proof faucet
  grease

Repair a washer-type faucet

A leaky faucet has a torturous way of wearing on nerves and water resources. Even a slow drip can waste hundreds of gallons per month. Luckily, most dripping washer-type faucets can be cured in 30 minutes for less than a dollar.

To repair a washer-type faucet, you'll need to replace the washer on the bottom of the valve stem and sometimes replace the valve seat as well. Replace washers for both the hot and cold water while you're at it, not just the one that's leaking.

....

1. Turn off the water-supply valves and close the sink stopper so small parts won't disappear down the drain.

2. Remove the screw that holds the handle and remove handle. Then loosen and remove packing nut counterclockwise with a wrench. Remove valve stem assembly. It should pop or screw off.

3. Remove the worn washer on the end of the valve

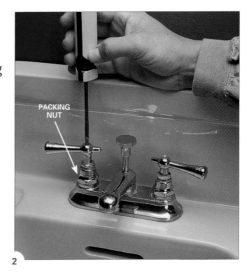

PACKING NUT

2

CAUTION:
Most faucet handles are secured by a screw, which is sometimes covered by a snap-on cap or button. You may need to tap, wiggle or pry the handle a bit to remove it.

pro tips!

➤ Take your worn washer and valve seat along to the home center or hardware store to find the exact matches.

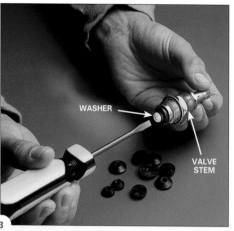

WASHER

VALVE STEM

3

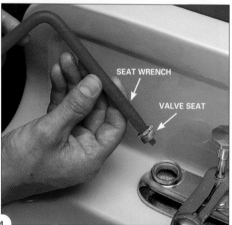

SEAT WRENCH

VALVE SEAT

4

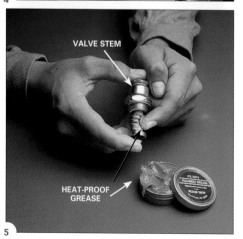

VALVE STEM

HEAT-PROOF GREASE

5

3. Remove the worn washer on the end of the valve stem and replace it with the correct type: flat or beveled. The new washer should fit snugly without being forced.

4. Use the seat wrench to remove worn valve seat. The new seat must match the old one exactly in diameter, height and number of threads.

5. Lubricate the working parts of the stem assembly with heat-proof faucet grease. Reassemble faucet.

pro tips!

➤ As you reassemble the faucet, dab a little grease on the screws and seat threads. They'll screw in more smoothly and come apart easier for future repairs.

CAUTION:
Check the owner's
manual or
manufacturer's
Web site to
confirm that
vinegar won't harm
the finish.

Unclog a showerhead

Over time, hard-water minerals in tap water build up and clog the spray holes in showerheads. Fix this problem by removing the showerhead and cleaning it.

1. Unscrew the showerhead by gripping the shower neck with a pipe wrench (as shown), grabbing the nut on the showerhead with the adjustable pliers and turning the pliers counterclockwise until the nut loosens. Protect the finishes on the showerhead and wall pipe by wrapping them with a cloth.

2. Open the showerhead holes by soaking the head overnight in a vinegar bath and poking the loosened mineral scale free with a toothpick. Rinse the showerhead in tap water, then reinstall it by applying Teflon tape to the wall pipe threads, screwing it on and tightening it by reversing the technique in Photo 1. Complete the repair by turning on the cold water in the shower and blasting out any remaining mineral gunk.

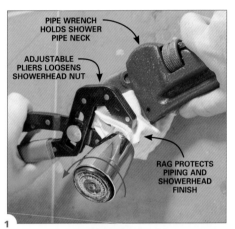

PIPE WRENCH HOLDS SHOWER PIPE NECK

ADJUSTABLE PLIERS LOOSENS SHOWERHEAD NUT

RAG PROTECTS PIPING AND SHOWERHEAD FINISH

1

VINEGAR BATH

2

pro tips!

➤ If the showerhead is too stuck to remove, try filling a plastic bag with vinegar, tying the top of the bag around the top of the showerhead and submerging it overnight in the vinegar.

Install scald protection

If the shower water in your bathroom or tub suddenly gets dangerously hot, you're not alone. Someone turning on water in the kitchen or flushing a toilet downstairs changes the water temperature for someone taking a shower upstairs. Scalding water is dangerous, especially for young kids who can't turn it off. Approximately 3,800 people are injured and 34 people die each year from excessively hot tap water, according to the Consumer Product Safety Commission.

Anti-scald valves have been required by code for years, but older homes may not have them. And putting them in an existing bathroom means tearing open the walls to access the plumbing pipes. An easier fix is to replace the showerhead and the tub spout with fixtures that have a built-in scald protection valve

PROFESSIONAL
COST: $150

YOUR COST: $50

SAVINGS: $100

COMPLEXITY
Simple

TOOLS
Long-handled
  adjustable pliers

MATERIALS
Pipe joint tape
Caulk (for tub spout)
Anti-scald valve

1. Unscrew the existing showerhead or tub spout, wrap pipe tape around the exposed threads, caulk around the opening for a tub spout, then attach the new fixture. When the water reaches an unsafe temperature, the fixture automatically cuts the water flow to a trickle. Flow resumes when the water cools. Codes may still require an anti-scald valve (not just an anti-scald fixture). Check with your local building inspector.

1

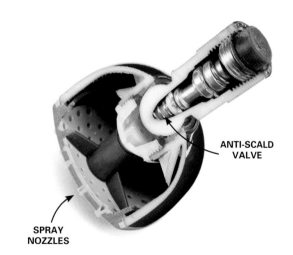

ANTI-SCALD
VALVE

SPRAY
NOZZLES

How to fix a leaking shutoff valve

Dripping shutoff valves can leave puddles of water on the bathroom floor. This quick DIY fix is something even a novice can handle.

The plumbing supply shutoff valves behind toilets or under sinks can go for years without being turned off and then reopened again. That inactivity can cause the neoprene washers to become brittle or crusted up with mineral deposits, and they lose their ability to seal leaks.

1. Tighten the packing nut on the toilet shutoff valve one-eighth turn clockwise to try to seal a leak around the nut. Wrap cloth or masking tape on the pliers' jaws to protect the nut's finish. Use light, steady pressure so you don't damage the water lines.

   If the neoprene washers are still flexible and clean, this should work to stop the leak.

WRAP MASKING TAPE ON JAWS OF PLIERS

ROTATE 1/8 TURN CLOCKWISE, GENTLY

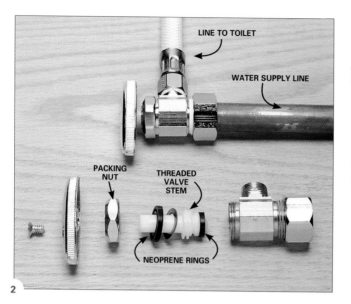

LINE TO TOILET

WATER SUPPLY LINE

PACKING NUT

THREADED VALVE STEM

NEOPRENE RINGS

2

pro tips!

➤ Properly sized replacement washers for the shutoff valve are available from plumbing supply houses and better hardware stores that stock a large inventory of repair parts.

2. If the leak persists, disassemble the shutoff valve. Turn off the house water main. Leave the toilet and supply lines intact. Unscrew the handle, the packing nut and the threaded valve stem. Clean the washers with a cloth and flex the neoprene to try to get it supple again. Avoid gumming up the inside of the shutoff valve; don't use any pipe dope or plastic tape on the valve stem's threads.

3. Reassemble the shutoff valve, turn the main house valve back on and check for leaks. If this step doesn't stop the leak, you'll need to replace the whole valve.

How to fix a clogged toilet

**PROFESSIONAL
COST:** $80

YOUR COST: $0

SAVINGS: $80

COMPLEXITY
Simple

TOOLS
Plunger with
flange-type cup
Closet auger or
plumbing snake

MATERIALS
Rubber gloves
Rags

CAUTION:
Wear rubber
gloves—things can
get messy.

A poor flush means that your toilet drain is either partially or completely plugged. A toilet that's completely plugged—a no-drainer—is obvious. The toilet bowl will fill to the brim with flush water and perhaps overflow. Give the water level 10 minutes or so to drop, then attack the problem with a plunger (Photo 1).

However, most clogged toilets are slow drainers, that is, flush water partially fills the bowl but doesn't rush out and clean away the waste. The water level remains high, then usually drains down to normal height within a minute or two. So if you suspect a problem, test the drainage first as we show in Photo 2.

1. Don't flush the toilet if you suspect a clog. Make a first plunge gently to expel air from the plunger bell; then plunge vigorously in and out. Keep the plunger covered with water. Stick with it, plunging 15 to 20 times if necessary. If the plunger fails to clear a clog, use a closet auger, as shown in Photo 3. Keep towels handy to wipe up water that splashes out.

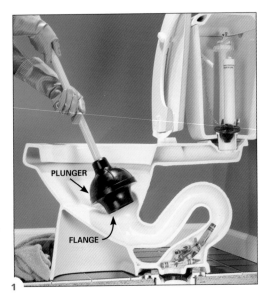

PLUNGER

FLANGE

1

pro tips!

➤ For about 90 percent of clogged toilets, you only need one special tool—a plunger. Buy one with an extension flange on the rubber bell-shaped end (Photo 1). It's designed to fit toilets better so you can deliver more "oomph" to the plunge. It'll unplug sink and tub drains too, if you simply fold the flange back into the bell.

CAUTION: Don't be suckered into thinking that powerful chemicals will do the messy work for you. They sometimes work, but they're slower. And when they don't work, you have a drain full of corrosive water on your hands. If you tried chemicals and they didn't work, run as much water into the toilet as possible and let it sit overnight to drain through the clog. Then, when you plunge, wear safety goggles and rubber gloves to keep the water out of your eyes and off your bare skin.

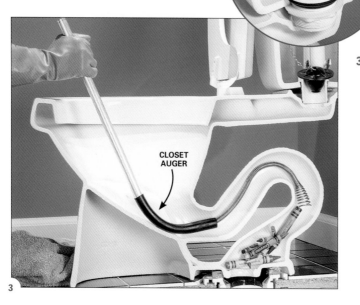

2. Test the drain by letting in small amounts of water—don't use the flush handle. Instead, remove the tank lid and lift the flapper valve slightly to let a cup or two of water into the bowl to see if the water goes down. If it's still plugged, you'll have to push the flapper down to restore the seal quickly. Flushing a clogged toilet may flood your floor!

FLAPPER

3. For stubborn clogs, spin a closet auger or regular snake through the drain. The hooked spring end should break through the clog or grab the obstruction (such as a rag) so you can pull it out. Once a clog passes the wax ring into the wider drain, it should move easily. If the clog resists all your efforts, you'll probably have to pull up the toilet.

CLOSET AUGER

pro tips!

➤ Even the least expensive snake will clear a toilet. But the closet auger (Photo 3) is a special type designed to get around the first bend, keep debris at arm's length, and still spin the coil to hook "foreign objects." A rubber sleeve protects the enamel bowl from scrape marks. These snakes are short because most obstructions catch in the first S-bend or at the floor flange. (Plumbers report that the most common foreign objects are toys.)

Toilet running— fix the flush valve

When a flush valve causes a toilet to run, a worn flapper is usually the culprit. But not always. First, look at the chain that raises the flapper. If there's too much slack in the chain, it can tangle up and prevent the flapper from closing firmly. A chain with too little slack can cause trouble too. Photo 3 shows how to set the slack just right.

1. Test the flapper. Push down on the flapper with a yardstick and listen. If the sound of running water stops, the flapper needs replacing.

Turn off the water, flush the toilet to empty the tank and then run your finger around the rim of the flush valve seat. If you feel mineral deposits, clean the flush valve seat with an abrasive sponge or ScotchBrite pad. Don't use anything that might roughen it. If cleaning the flush valve seat doesn't solve the problem, you need to replace the flapper.

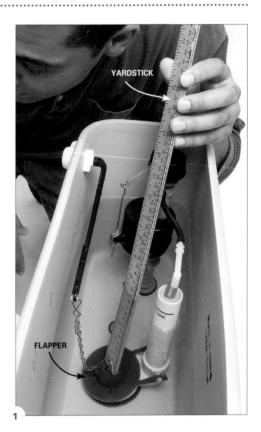

YARDSTICK

FLAPPER

1

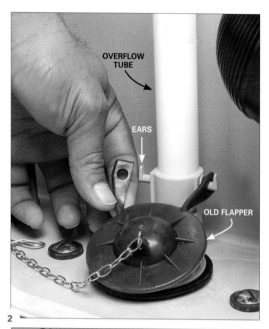

OVERFLOW TUBE

EARS

OLD FLAPPER

2

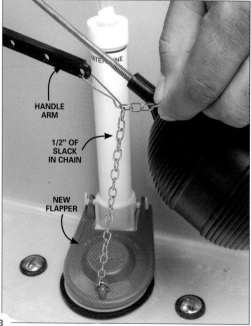

HANDLE ARM

1/2" OF SLACK IN CHAIN

NEW FLAPPER

3

2. Remove the old flapper from the ears of the overflow tube and detach the chain from the handle arm.

3. Attach the new flapper to the overflow tube and hook the chain to the handle arm. Leave 1/2 in. of slack in the chain. Turn the water back on and test-flush the toilet.

pro tips!

➤ Your flapper may screw onto a threaded rod or have a ring that slips over the overflow tube. If you have an unusual flush valve, finding a replacement flapper may be the hardest part of the job.

To find a suitable replacement, turn off the water, remove the old flapper and take it to a home center or hardware store. You may not find an identical match, but chances are you'll locate one of the same shape and diameter. If not, try a plumbing supply store or search online.

It helps to know the brand and model of your toilet. The brand name is usually on the bowl behind the seat. In some cases, the model or number will be on the underside of the lid or inside the tank. Matching an unusual flapper can become a trial-and-error process.

PROFESSIONAL
COST: $80

YOUR COST: $0

SAVINGS: $80

COMPLEXITY
Simple

TOOLS
4-in-1 screwdriver
Drill/driver, cordless
Drill bit set
Pliers

MATERIALS
Toilet seat
 tightening kit
Toilet seat
 stabilizer kit

Toilet seat repair

Tighten a loose or wiggly toilet seat with inexpensive rubber bushings and seat stabilizers. It's a 15-minute fix that'll last for years.

1. Slide on a rubber bushing from the toilet seat tightening kit, with the tapered side facing up toward the toilet seat. Then use the tightening tool from the kit to snug up the nut.

2. Loop the rubber bands around the toilet seat from the stabilizer kit, and center the stabilizers so they touch the inside rim of the bowl. Drill a starter hole and secure the stabilizers with screws from the kit.

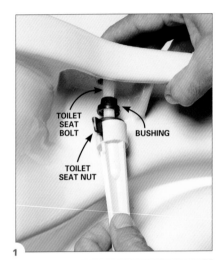

TOILET
SEAT
BOLT

BUSHING

TOILET
SEAT NUT

1

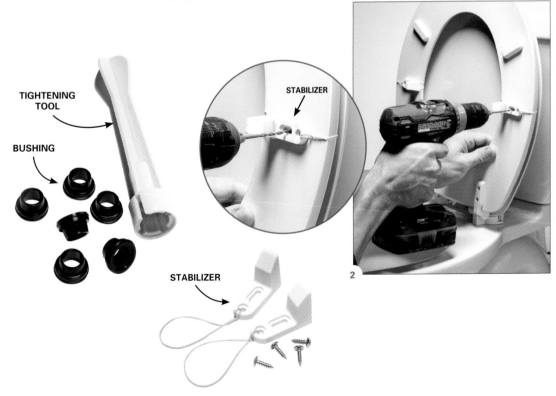

TIGHTENING
TOOL

BUSHING

STABILIZER

STABILIZER

2

Quick fix for a sluggish toilet

If your poorly flushing toilet worked well in the past and you live in an area with hard water, chances are the rinse holes around the bottom of the rim have become clogged with lime deposits. Clear rinse and siphon holes are crucial for complete flushing action. Even though the water from the tank will eventually find its way into the bowl, high water volume on the first surge is important for good flushing. There has to be a "critical mass" of water for solids to be flushed.

1. Use a hand mirror to see the holes under the rim of the toilet. Bend a coat hanger flat and probe the tip into the holes to poke out any mineral deposits.

2. Dry the bottom of the rim, then roll up paper towel "ropes" and seal them against the bottom of the rinse holes with plumber's putty pushed against the bottom of the rim. Seal the siphon jet hole with another glob of putty.

3. Pour a bottle of lime remover into the overflow pipe. Let it sit for an hour (or recommended time on product) to allow the lime remover to dissolve deposits. Remove everything and flush the toilet several times.

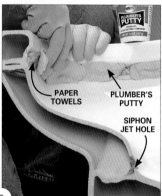

1

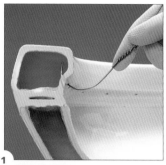

PAPER TOWELS

PLUMBER'S PUTTY

SIPHON JET HOLE

2

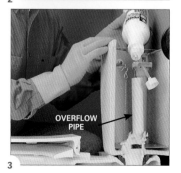

OVERFLOW PIPE

3

PROFESSIONAL COST: $80

YOUR COST: $0

SAVINGS: $80

COMPLEXITY
Simple

TOOLS
Coat hanger

MATERIALS
Plumber's putty
Paper towels
Lime remover

CAUTION:
Wear rubber gloves—things can get messy.

How to fix sweating pipes

If your cold water pipes are sweating more than you are on these hot summer days, here's the simple cure. Run down to the local home center, lumberyard or hardware store and pick up some foam pipe insulation.

The deluxe version we purchased has a peel-and-stick seam along its length. Less expensive insulation lacks this feature, but you can tape the seam to seal it. We also bought a roll of peel-and-stick seam sealer to wrap around the joints between tubes. The insulation is available in different sizes, so you'll need to measure the diameter and total length of the pipes you intend to insulate.

The insulated tubing keeps the warm, humid air from condensing on the cold pipes. Insulating hot water pipes offers little advantage beyond the possibility of getting hot water sooner at faucets far from the water heater.

1. Measure the length of pipe and cut insulation to length with a serrated bread knife.

2. Miter the corners and cut a V-shaped notch where pipes intersect at a "T," using a utility knife.

3. Seal joints between lengths of tubing with special "peel-and-stick" seam-sealing tape or foil duct tape.

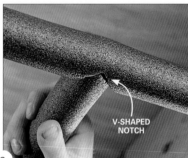

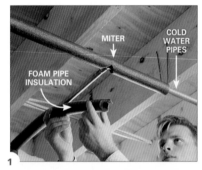

Stop a small plumbing leak

Small water leaks at soldered copper joints can be easy to fix. Just take a little extra care in cleaning and fluxing the joints. Leaks in newly soldered copper pipes are rare.

1. Drain the water before you solder. Shut off the water at the main valve in your home and open up nearby faucets to completely drain the pipe with the leaky elbow.

2. Dry the outside of the elbow and sand (120-grit paper or cloth) around the leaking joint to remove all surface corrosion.

3. Apply soldering flux around the whole joint and apply heat with a torch until the old solder melts.

4. Add new solder until a shiny ring of solder shows all around the joint. It's easier to reach around the backside of the joint if you bend a hook on the end of the solder before you start. Heat the joint just enough to melt the solder. (When the copper is hot enough, the solder will melt like butter. If

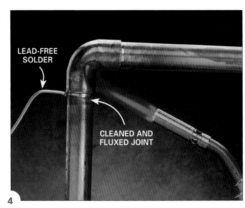

LEAD-FREE SOLDER

CLEANED AND FLUXED JOINT

4

the solder beads up and rolls off rather than flowing, you've probably burned the flux or the copper isn't clean enough.) Let the pipe cool for five minutes, then turn the water back on and cross your fingers that you stopped the leak.

PROFESSIONAL COST: $150

YOUR COST: $40

SAVINGS: $110

COMPLEXITY
Simple

TOOLS
Slip-joint pliers
Soldering torch
Tube cutter

MATERIALS
Plumber's tape
Rags
120-grit sandpaper
  or cloth
Lead-free solder
Flux
Copper pipe
Copper fittings

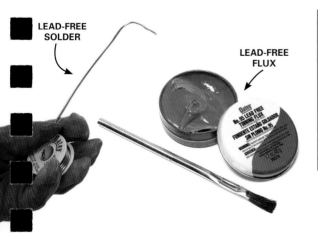

LEAD-FREE SOLDER

LEAD-FREE FLUX

CAUTION:
Avoid fires when working with a flaming torch (especially when the water is turned off). Fill a bucket with water first to have nearby. It is also a good idea to keep a fire extinguisher handy.
  Don't solder close to wood or other flammable material without protecting it from the flame.

SELF-LIGHTING TORCH

PROFESSIONAL
COST: $150

YOUR COST: $30

SAVINGS: $120

COMPLEXITY
Simple

TOOLS
Adjustable wrench

MATERIALS
2 water hammer
  arresters
Bucket
Rags

Stop banging water lines on your washing machine

If your plumbing bangs and clangs like a truckload of scrap metal, you've got "water hammer." Water develops momentum as it flows fast through pipes. When a valve closes quickly and stops the flow, that momentum shakes and pounds pipes. Water hammer arresters cure this condition with a cushion of air that absorbs the momentum.

Washing machines have screw-on connections, making them as easy to attach as a garden hose.

CAUTION:
Make sure to measure your pipes before purchase to get the correct size water arresters— 1/2 in. or 3/4.

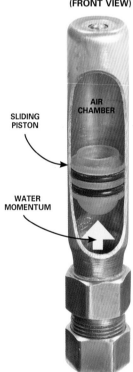

WATER HAMMER
ARRESTER
(FRONT VIEW)

SLIDING
PISTON

AIR
CHAMBER

WATER
MOMENTUM

THE SLIDING PISTON ABSORBS SUDDEN
PRESSURE CHANGES AND KEEPS THE
PIPES FROM BANGING.

1. Turn off water supply at the washing machine valves. Place a bucket under washer hoses to catch any remaining water in the lines. Disconnect the washer hoses from the water supply valves. Take care that the washers at the end of the hoses do not fall off.

2. Dry connections with rags. Screw on the water hammer arresters clockwise to each water supply valve, hot and cold. (Check the packaging for installation details.) Make sure that there are washers in the swivel nuts. Secure connection by tightening with an adjustable wrench.

WATER
HAMMER
ARRESTERS

MAKE SURE WASHERS
ARE IN SWIVEL NUTS

WASHER
HOSES

3. Connect the washer hoses to the water hammer arresters. Again, make sure the washers are in the swivel nuts.

4. Turn the water back on and check for leaks. Tighten any joints that may be leaking just a bit.

PROFESSIONAL
COST: $200

YOUR COST: $20

SAVINGS: $180

COMPLEXITY
Simple

TOOLS
4-in-1 screwdriver

MATERIALS
Safety glasses
Broom
Bucket
Toothbrush

> **CAUTION:**
> Don't use rock salt;
> it contains dirt and
> other impurities
> that can clog
> the softener.

Instant water softener fixes

Is your soft water not so soft anymore? You can often fix the problem yourself. However, if you have an older softener (20 years or so) and none of these fixes work, it may need replacement

---

1. Set the water supply to bypass.

Put on safety glasses. Check for salt problems in the brine tank. Start by pushing a broom handle down into the salt to break up salt bridges (like a dome), blocking salt from dropping to the bottom of the tank. If too little salt gets dissolved, the resin bed won't get clean and the water won't get softened.

When the salt level is low (or at least once a year), check for a crust of salt mush at the bottom. This thick salt paste doesn't dissolve well, reducing the salinity of the brine solution, and needs to be removed.

Scoop out the mush at the bottom of the tank, then pour in hot water to dissolve the rest before regenerating the system.

SALT MUSH

1

pro tips!

➤ Before you tear apart your softener, check the control settings—especially after a long power outage. The timer clock has to show the right time so that the resin tank is cleaned and recharged when no one is using water (usually early morning).

Also make sure the hardness setting is still correct—well-water hardness can change over time. Bring a small container of your water to a water softener dealer for a water hardness test, then check the results against your settings.

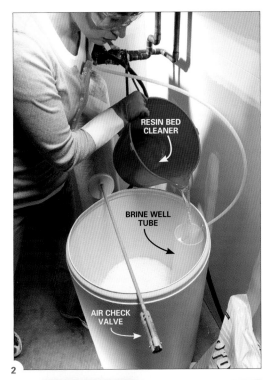

RESIN BED CLEANER

BRINE WELL TUBE

AIR CHECK VALVE

2

pro tips!

➤ Clean the resin bed twice a year with resin bed cleaner (available at water softener dealers) if you have "clear water iron" (dissolved iron makes a glass of water turn cloudy or rusty after sitting for several minutes). Otherwise the resin bed won't remove the iron.

2. Pour diluted resin cleaner into the brine well tube. Lift out the air check valve (or brine valve assembly) and clean it in warm water.

3. Unscrew and remove the cap that covers the venturi assembly and filter screen and carefully remove the parts.

4. Gently clean dirt and mineral deposits from the screen and from the venturi assembly parts in a pan of warm water. (The salty water flows through these parts from the brine tank to the resin tank. If the screen and nozzle get clogged by sediment, the resin bed won't be cleaned and the water will stay hard).

   Turn on water supply and run the hot water after you turn the softener back on to flush out any hard water.

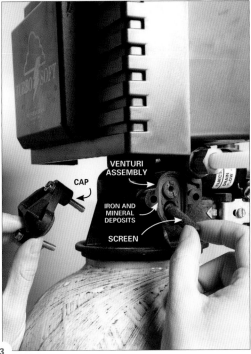

CAP

VENTURI ASSEMBLY

IRON AND MINERAL DEPOSITS

SCREEN

3

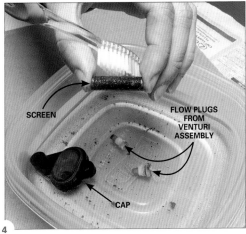

SCREEN

FLOW PLUGS FROM VENTURI ASSEMBLY

CAP

4

Chapter 4
Appliances

PROFESSIONAL
COST: $90

YOUR COST: $0

SAVINGS: $90

COMPLEXITY
Simple

TOOLS
Level
Screwdriver
Putty knife if required
Hairdryer

MATERIALS
3 quarters
Sponge
Flexible tubing that
 fits into drain hole

CAUTION:
Check your
owner's manual for
drain tube location
on your fridge.

Fix a leaking fridge

The water supply lines that serve icemakers or water dispensers can leak and make pools under the fridge. But a fridge without these features can create water problems, too. Every fridge produces water in the form of condensation and melting ice. When the system that deals with this water fails, you can end up with puddles inside and outside of the fridge.

Water drains into a pan under the fridge where it evaporates. If your fridge is badly tilted, water can spill out of the pan. Leveling the fridge solves this problem.

If the drain tube in the freezer gets plugged, water leaks into the compartment below or onto the floor.

1. Adjust the fridge so it's level from side to side and tilted backward. Stack quarters near the back and set a 2-ft. level on them. When the bubble shows level, the tilt is correct.

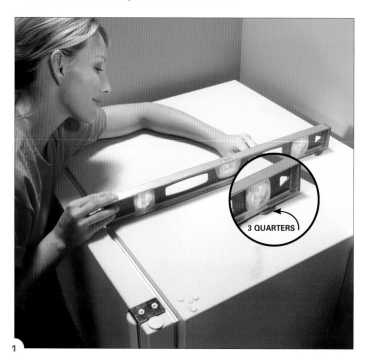

3 QUARTERS

1

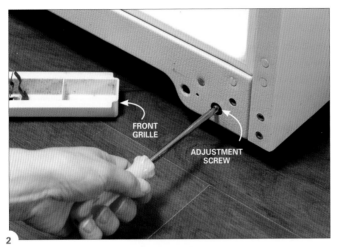

FRONT GRILLE

ADJUSTMENT SCREW

2

2. Pull off the front cover grille to level or tilt the fridge. Turn adjustment screws to raise or lower the front corners of the fridge.

3. To clear the drain tub, remove the screws that hold the back cover panel in place. On some models, you have to pry out plastic screw covers with a putty knife to expose the screws. Use a hair dryer to melt any ice buildup. Sop away the melt water with a sponge. Then clean up around the drain hole.

4. Insert a tube in the drain hole and blow out any debris. Any tube that fits tightly into the hole will work. Pour a 1/2 cup of water into the tube to make sure it drains before you replace the cover panel.

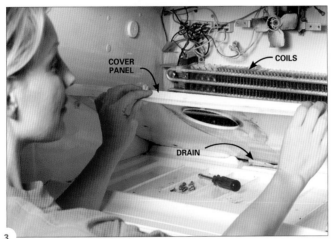

COVER PANEL

COILS

DRAIN

3

DRAIN HOLE

4

Straighten sagging refrigerator doors with two turns of a wrench!

Straighten a crooked fridge door in less than five minutes. You save money by stopping cool air leaks around the door.

A sagging refrigerator or freezer door doesn't just look bad. It can cause the door gaskets to seal poorly, and that means your fridge will work harder to keep the milk cold. It can also lead to frost buildup in the freezer.

1. To realign the door, just pry off the hinge cap and loosen the hinge bolts slightly with a wrench.

2. Then align the door with the top of the refrigerator. Adjust only the top hinge to straighten an upper door. To realign the lower door, adjust the middle hinge. Moving the middle hinge will affect the upper door, so you may have to adjust the top hinge afterward. Retighten the bolts.

Clear and clean refrigerator drip openings

Drip openings allow water that has melted from the defrost cycle to flow down to a pan located by the compressor, where it evaporates. Check your owner's manual for the location on your fridge. On cycle defrost fridges, a channel directs the water to a tube in the food compartment (see below). On frost-free types, look for a small cap under the crisper drawers that covers a hole, or an opening in the back of the freezer or refrigerator. If the drain opening clogs, water will build up under the crisper drawers and eventually pour out onto the floor.

1. Locate the drip opening and wipe it out, being careful not to press any debris down into the hole. Suck out crumbs with a vacuum.

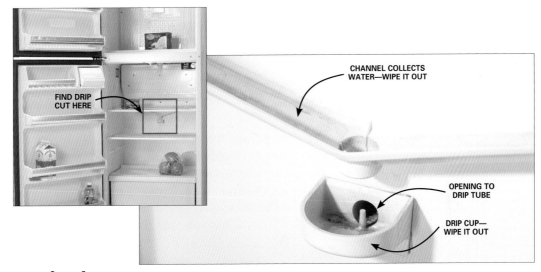

FIND DRIP CUT HERE

CHANNEL COLLECTS WATER—WIPE IT OUT

OPENING TO DRIP TUBE

DRIP CUP— WIPE IT OUT

pro tips!

➤ **Is your freezer full of frost?** Check the freezer door. Frost is a sure sign that the freezer door is ajar. All it takes is one too many cartons of ice cream to hold the door open a crack. Rearrange the freezer contents so the door closes completely and you may save on a service call.

SAVINGS: $75

COMPLEXITY
Simple

TOOLS
Coil-cleaning brush
Vacuum

CAUTION:
Shut power off on the refrigerator by unplugging or switching off the circuit breaker before cleaning the coils or fan.

Fridge or freezer won't cool

There are lots of malfunctions that can take the chill out of your fridge. One common cause of suddenly soft ice cream or warm juice is a simple loss of electricity. If the light doesn't come on when you open the fridge door, make sure the fridge is plugged in and check the breaker panel. If the fridge runs but doesn't get cold enough, chances are one of the following fixes will restore the chill.

1. Check the temperature control dial. The temperature control dial inside the fridge is sometimes irresistible to curious kids. Make sure it hasn't been turned way down. Adjust the temperature control dial.

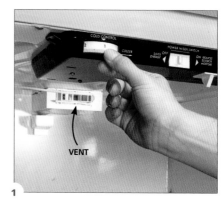

2. Make sure the vents inside the fridge or freezer compartment aren't blocked by containers. These little vents on frost-free fridges allow air to circulate in the freezer. Don't block them or let crumbs or twist ties get sucked in around the evaporator fan or clog the drain tube. To help save energy, keep your freezer about three-quarters full to retain cold air. But don't pack it any fuller—the air needs to circulate.

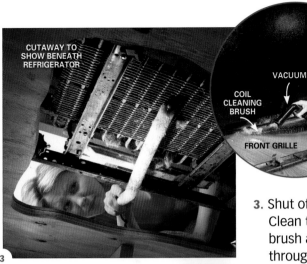

CUTAWAY TO SHOW BENEATH REFRIGERATOR

COIL CLEANING BRUSH

VACUUM

FRONT GRILLE

3

CONDENSER FAN

COVER PANEL

4

3. Shut off power to the refrigerator. Clean the coils with a coil-cleaning brush and vacuum so air can flow through them. In order for your fridge to create a chill, air has to flow freely through the condenser coils. A coil-cleaning brush, which is bendable to fit in tight areas, does a thorough job.

4. With refrigerator off, free up the condenser fan. Pull out the fridge and unscrew the cover panel. Vacuum the fan. Then start the refrigerator to make sure the fan turns freely.

COIL-CLEANING BRUSH

pro tips!

➤ On most older refrigerators, the coils are on the backside. Cereal boxes on top of the fridge or grocery bags stuffed behind it can reduce the needed airflow.

➤ Most newer refrigerators have coils underneath, where they can get blocked by trash and plugged with dust. The result is your compressor works harder and longer than it was designed to, using more energy and shortening the life of your fridge.

➤ Even if your fridge is working fine, you should pull off the front grille and clean the coils every year for efficient operation; do it every six months if you have shedding pets.

PROFESSIONAL
COST: $115

YOUR COST: $0

SAVINGS: $115

COMPLEXITY
Simple

TOOLS
4-in-1 screwdriver
Wire brush
Small screwdriver

MATERIALS
Replacement parts,
 if needed

> **CAUTION:**
> Always unplug
> your electric range
> before removing a
> burner.

Repair an electric range burner that won't heat

If your range has a burner that's not working, chances are you can fix it without any special tools. To diagnose a burner problem, go through the steps in order. If the burners still don't work, call a service professional for help. Our list should take care of 95 percent of the problems that could occur with a burner. If you see burned wires, have a pro look at the range. It could indicate a bigger problem.

1. Unplug the range. Remove the bad burner. Compare the nonfunctioning burner with the other burners. If it looks pitted and scorched, slip the burner out of its socket and replace it. To remove a burner, simply lift it slightly and pull the prongs from the socket. You may have to wiggle it slightly to get the prongs to release. Some burners are held by a screw that you must remove.

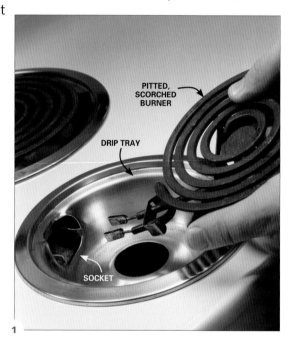

PITTED, SCORCHED BURNER

DRIP TRAY

SOCKET

1

pro tips!

➤ **Tips for buying replacement parts**
Before you go to purchase a part, write down the brand name, model number and serial number of the range. The range will have an engraved plate with this information usually located under the cooktop lid or on the back. Look in the Yellow Pages under "Appliances, Parts" for a supplier. Call first to be sure the part you need is in stock. Or order over the Internet.

TERMINALS

2. Tighten a burner connection. Wiggle the burner in the socket. If it's loose in the socket, pull it out and spread the burner terminals slightly for a tighter connection. Do this gently—the metal is fragile and you don't want to crack the heating element! Then clean the socket with a wire brush. Reinstall the burner, plug the stove back in and test the results.

3. Remove a functioning burner of the same size and try it in the socket that's not working. If that burner works, replace the bad burner with a new one.

4. Inspect the burner socket. If it's charred or scorched, replace it by removing the screws that secure it to the range top. Then unscrew the range wires and screw them to the terminals on the new socket. There are two main types of wire connections. Sockets have either screw connections or wire leads that you attach to the range wiring with the supplied ceramic wire connectors.

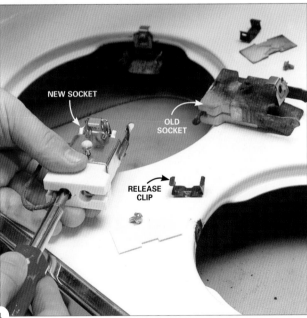

NEW SOCKET

OLD SOCKET

RELEASE CLIP

PROFESSIONAL
COST: $115

YOUR COST: $0

SAVINGS: $115

COMPLEXITY
Simple

TOOLS
Old toothbrush
Needle

Gas range won't light? Clean the igniter

A one-minute cleaning will solve 75 percent of burner problems. To get at the ignition system, lift the lid of your stove. Give it a rap with the heel of your hand if it's stuck. If your stove has sealed burners, identified by the igniter or little nub at the back of each burner, the lid won't lift. But you can clean the igniter the same way.

1. Access the pilot or igniter. Lift the hinged top. Most stove tops lift up. However, stoves with sealed burners don't have tops that lift.

2. To access the ignition system in an older-style standard gas range, pop the lid. If the pilot flame is out, poke a needle into the pilot hole to clean out soot (be careful not to ream it wider). Brush off any debris and clean the tube that leads from the pilot to the burner. Then relight the pilot. Lower the lid and turn on your burners to test them.

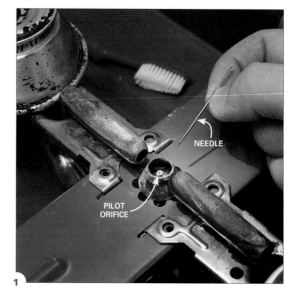

NEEDLE

PILOT
ORIFICE

1

CAUTION:
All the repairs and cleaning that we show can be safely done without shutting off the gas to the stove. But don't leave a burner dial on. It'll emit gas into the room. If at any time you smell gas, turn off the gas at the shutoff behind the range or at the main supply near the meter and ventilate the room. Then call your local utility or a service professional for assistance. (Look under "Appliances, Service and Repair" in your Yellow Pages.)

IGNITER

IGNITER

ROUND
CERAMIC
SEAL

2

IGNITER

NO GAP
AROUND
BURNER

3

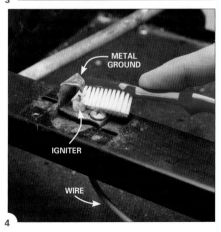

METAL
GROUND

IGNITER

WIRE

4

2. On electronic ignition stoves, it's a little ceramic nub located on the stovetop or under the ceramic seal strike plate. Also make sure that the round ceramic seal strike plate is properly sealed on the burner.

3. On a sealed burner, clean the igniter the same way.

4. On spark ignitions, clean the metal "ground" above the igniter wire, too. It must be clean to conduct a spark. Close the lid and turn the burner knob to "Light" to test the burner. It clicks when it's working.

PROFESSIONAL
COST: $100

YOUR COST: $0

SAVINGS: $100

COMPLEXITY
Simple

MATERIALS
Instruction manual

How to adjust oven temperatures

If the temperature in your oven doesn't match your temperature setting, or if your new oven just doesn't cook like your old one, you can recalibrate the temperature setting. The instructions for adjusting the temperature are in your instruction manual. If you don't have a manual, ask the manufacturer to send you one or go online and search for a downloadable version. Enter your oven's model number along with the words "instruction manual" in the search box and you're sure to find what you need.

You'll need a good-quality oven thermometer to see if your oven is heating accurately. (We show an OXO brand). Check local retailers (kitchen and department stores tend to carry good ones) or buy one online.

1. Set a thermometer in the oven on the center shelf and let the oven heat to a constant temperature.

2. Adjust the temperature setting using the procedure outlined in your manual to match the temperature setting to the thermometer reading. On this GE oven, you press the "bake" and "broil" buttons simultaneously, and then press "bake" to enter the temperature-adjusting mode. Then you keep pressing the "+" or "- " button to coordinate the thermostat with the actual oven temperature.

1

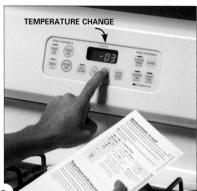
2

Remove scratches from stainless steel appliances

Stainless steel is a great look until you scratch it. Then it looks awful. Buff out ugly scratches in your shiny stainless steel appliances using fine sandpaper and rubbing compound.

PROFESSIONAL
COST: $150

YOUR COST: $6

SAVINGS: $144

COMPLEXITY
Simple

TOOLS
Sanding block
 (400- to 600-grit)
Abrasive pad

MATERIALS
Rubbing compound
Stainless steel
 cleaner/polish
(Or a repair kit with
 everything you
 need)

1. Start with the finest grit sandpaper or pad and zigzag a stream of sanding fluid (or rubbing compound) on it. Then gently sand the scratched area. Determine the direction of the "grain" and sand in one direction only, following the brushed pattern. Don't sand back and forth and never sand against the "grain."

   If the scratch won't come out after sanding for a few minutes, move up to the next coarsest grit.

2. When the scratch disappears, sand the rest of the panel until it blends in.

   You'll have to develop a feel for the technique, so start on an inconspicuous area of the appliance panel.

3. Finish by applying a stainless steel cleaner/polish.

1

GRAIN

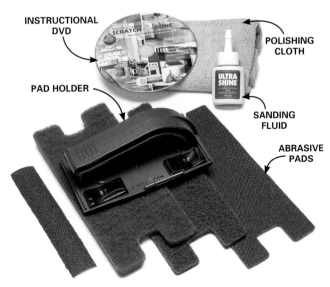

INSTRUCTIONAL DVD

PAD HOLDER

POLISHING CLOTH

SANDING FLUID

ABRASIVE PADS

CAUTION:
The sanding technique only works on plain (uncoated) stainless steel panels. Never try this procedure on simulated stainless steel or stainless panels with a fingerprint-resistant clear coat.
 Hint: If your appliance fingerprints easily, chances are it's plain stainless steel.

Dishwasher not cleaning dishes—try these solutions

When your dishwasher doesn't clean well, fix it yourself following these simple steps and avoid the expensive professional service call. A simple cleaning often solves the problem. Start by consulting your manual to be sure you're using the right detergent, loading the dishes correctly and maintaining the right hot water temperature.

1. Pull out the lower rack and remove the spray arm. This also allows access to the filter for cleaning. Some spray arms simply snap off, others require you to unscrew a cap on top.

SPRAY ARM

1

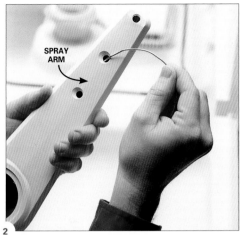

SPRAY ARM

2. Clean out the holes with a small wire.

3. Remove the filter screen if possible. Otherwise, use a wet/ dry vacuum to suck out the debris.

4. Make sure the float moves up and down freely. If the float on your dishwasher is removable, take the float apart and clean it. Jiggle it gently up and down.

pro tips!

➤ Insufficient water in the dishwasher also can cause poor cleaning. If the float gets stuck in the raised position, the dishwasher won't fill with water. To determine if your dishwasher is getting enough water, start a wash cycle. Open the door when you hear the machine stop filling. The water should reach or come close to the heating coil. If it doesn't, first make sure the float valve is operating freely (Photo 4).

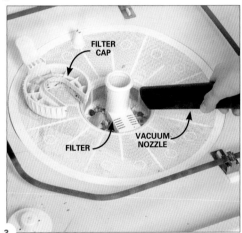

FILTER CAP

FILTER

VACUUM NOZZLE

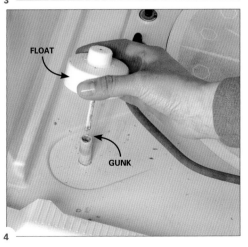

FLOAT

GUNK

> **CAUTION:**
> Don't reach for
> the bleach bottle.
> Bleach is very
> corrosive to metal
> parts.

How to fix a smelly dishwasher

If you smell bad dishwasher odors after running a cycle, don't reach for the bleach bottle. Bleach is very corrosive to metal parts and doesn't solve the root problem. The smell comes from bacteria that feed on trapped food and grease in the strainer screen at the bottom of the machine, in the jets in the sprayer arms and along the bottom edge of the door.

1. Start by cleaning and rinsing out the filter screen at the bottom of the dishwasher. Wet/dry vacuums work very well.

2. Next, clean out any food lodged in the sprayer arm ports. Poke food particles from the holes with a flexible wire.

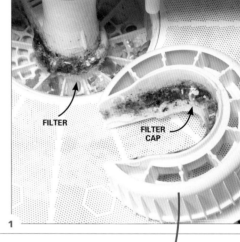

FILTER

FILTER
CAP

1

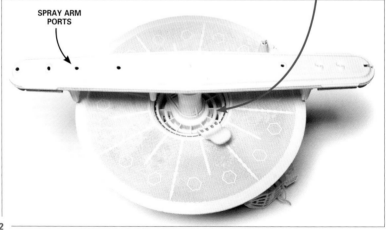

SPRAY ARM
PORTS

2

FOOD BUILDUP

3

3. Clean the door lip. Tip the door down all the way and spray the bottom edge and lip area with cleaner/degreaser spray. Let it soak for a while, then scrub it clean. Repeat any time you see buildup.

4. Once you've cleaned those areas, throw in a bottle of dishwasher cleaner and disinfectant (Dishwasher Magic; order from amazon.com) and run a full cycle with no dishes or dishwashing detergent. Keep those critical areas clean in the future and your stinking problem won't come back.

Garbage disposer fixes

When you flip the switch to turn on the garbage disposer and all you get is a hum—or a loud, metal-on-metal grinding noise—you know something's wrong. It might be revived with a simple fix. Here are three things to try.

1. If your garbage disposer is hard-wired, start by flipping off the circuit breaker. If it plugs in, unplug it.

   Look for a jam. Something too tough to grind, such as a piece of glass, could be jamming the motor. Remove the rubber baffle inside the drain—most just lift out—and shine a flashlight into the hole. Fish out the obstruction with a pair of tongs or needle-nose pliers.

2. Turn the motor manually. You'll need a hex wrench. Some disposers come with one bent at a convenient angle, but if you don't have it, you can buy one at a hardware store or use a standard Allen wrench. Rotate the wrench back and forth as shown until the motor turns a full revolution, then remove the wrench and switch on the motor.

ALLEN
WRENCH

2

RESET
BUTTON

3

3. Press the reset button. If your motor has overheated by working too long, wait five minutes for it to cool down, then push the reset button. (It's usually located on the underside of the disposer.) The motor may also have overheated because of a jam. If the motor doesn't start after manually turning it, try pushing the reset button. Turn on a cold stream of water and turn the disposer switch to "on" position; the disposer should now run again.

PROFESSIONAL
COST: $150

YOUR COST: $0

SAVINGS: $150

COMPLEXITY
Simple

TOOLS
4-in-1 screwdriver

MATERIALS
New splash guard
Stack of books
Block of wood
Shims

> **CAUTION:**
> Unplug garbage
> disposer or flip off
> the circuit breaker.

How to replace a garbage disposer splash guard

Got a garbage disposer that spits, um, garbage at you? Forget about replacing the entire unit. You can install a new splash guard in about 20 minutes. You don't need any special tools.

1. If your garbage disposer is hard-wired, start by flipping off the circuit breaker. If it plugs in, unplug it. Assemble a support for the disposer by stacking up some books and a piece of wood on top. Then unscrew and remove the drainpipe.

2. To disconnect the disposer, jam a screwdriver into the locking ring and rotate it away from you. That will release the collar and the disposer will drop onto the books. Support it with one hand so it doesn't tip over.

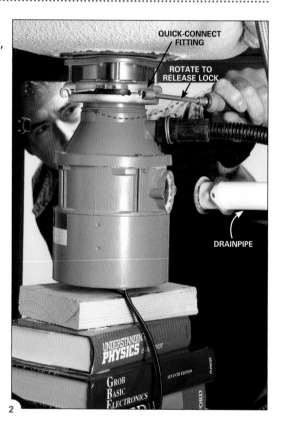

QUICK-CONNECT FITTING

ROTATE TO RELEASE LOCK

DRAINPIPE

2

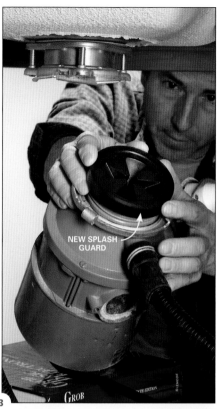

NEW SPLASH GUARD

3

3. Remove the top piece of wood from the bookstack to lower the disposer enough to replace the splash guard. Grab the lower edge of the old rubber guard and peel it up and off. Then slip the new one on and push it down until it seats.

4. Reconnect the disposer by replacing the wood piece and adding several shims between the books and the bottom of the disposer until the locking ring just touches the sink flange. Then just rotate the ring to lock it in place. Reinstall the drain line, do a leak test and grind away.

pro tips!

➤ The hardest part of reinstallation is hoisting the disposer up and into place with one hand while you try to engage the locking ring with the other. Shoving several shims between the books and the bottom of disposer make the process go smoothly.

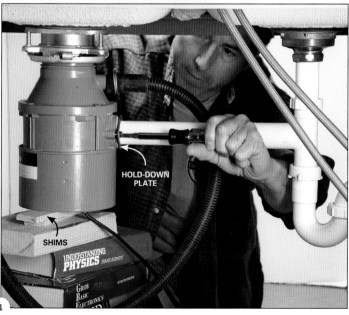

HOLD-DOWN PLATE

SHIMS

4

PROFESSIONAL
COST: $75

YOUR COST: $0

SAVINGS: $75

COMPLEXITY
Simple

TOOLS
Level
Pry bar
Wrench

MATERIALS
Block of wood

Quiet a noisy washer

When a washing machine cabinet rocks, it makes a horrible racket during the spin cycle. The solution is to simply readjust the legs. Fortunately, it's an easy fix, though you may need a helper to tilt up the machine.

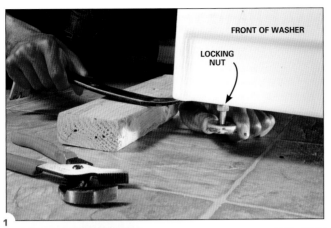

FRONT OF WASHER

LOCKING
NUT

1. Lift the machine slightly with a pry bar to take the weight off the front legs, then turn the legs until the side of the washer is plumb. Adjust the front legs to make the machine level across the front and from front to back. The legs can usually be turned by hand after the locking nut at the top of the threads is turned down, but if the threads are rusted, use a wrench.

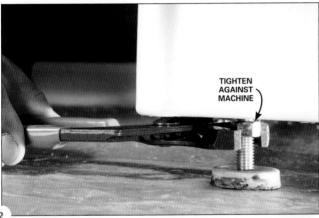

TIGHTEN
AGAINST
MACHINE

2. After leveling, lock the leg into place. Tighten the locking nut up against the frame of the washing machine to keep the leg from turning.

SELF-
LEVELING
SUPPORT

TAP LEGS
TO LOOSEN

3. Most washing machines have self-adjusting rear legs that level from side to side, but dirt, lint and rust may keep them from working properly. If the back isn't level, tip the washing machine up a few inches and then set it back down so the weight of the machine loosens the legs. If the machine still doesn't level out, the self-leveling support may be rusted against the washing machine frame. Tip the machine off the ground, then break the self-leveling support loose by tapping the legs.

Fix a slow-filling washer

A washing machine that takes forever to fill may have an inlet screen clogged with mineral deposits and tiny particles of debris. These screens catch debris in the water supply and protect a washer's internal parts. Often, screens clog after a remodeling project or after work by city crews on water mains. Any work on water lines can loosen sediment in pipes and lead to plugged screens.

Cleaning the screens is a simple job. The only tricky part is removing the screens without wrecking them (Photos 1 and 2). Don't just yank them out. Gently squeeze and twist as you pull. You'll distort the screens a little, but you can mold them back into shape with your fingers. If your screens are cemented in place by mineral deposits, you may not be able to remove them without damage. New screens are inexpensive and are sold at appliance parts stores.

1. **Disconnect hoses**. Turn off the hot and cold water supplies and disconnect the hoses. Use a pair of needle-nose pliers to gently remove the screens for cleaning.

1

DIRTY SCREEN

2

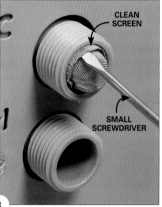

CLEAN SCREEN

SMALL SCREWDRIVER

3

2. Clean the dirty inlet screen with running water or blow out debris with an air compressor.

3. Reinsert the screen. Work the clean screen back into the inlet by pressing around the rim of the screen with a small screwdriver.

4. Check your washer supply hoses, too. Some contain screens that can be removed and cleaned just like inlet screens. Reconnect the hoses, turn on the water and check for leaks.

HOSE SCREEN

pro tips!

➤ If your washing machine is connected to bare rubber hoses, you're risking thousands of dollars' worth of water damage. Under constant water pressure, these hoses are prone to leaks or even bursting. That's why building codes say that the water supply should be shut off when the washer isn't in use—unless it's connected to no-burst hoses.

   No-burst hoses are encased in a woven metal sleeve that prevents weak spots in the rubber from developing into leaks. The hoses are available at home centers, and installing them is as easy as connecting a garden hose.

PROFESSIONAL
COST: $75

YOUR COST: $0

SAVINGS: $75

COMPLEXITY
Simple

TOOLS
4-in-1 screwdriver

MATERIALS
Wood block

Front-loading washer won't drain

A front-loading washing machine that won't drain may need nothing more than a simple filter cleaning, especially if it's a Maytag. Learn how to access the filter and how to clean it.

Even though some instruction manuals don't mention it, there's a filter near the water pump that catches stuff before it gets into the pump and causes damage. If the filter gets clogged, it can prevent your machine from draining. In some cases, a code number will show up on the digital display. If you look up the code in the instruction manual, it will indicate a problem with suds or tell you to check the filter. On Maytag front loaders, it's easy to avoid these problems by cleaning the filter every six months. On newer Maytag machines, you can access the filter easily by removing the front panel. On Frigidaire and some other brands, the filter is part of the pump and you'll have to remove a hose or the entire pump to clean it.

1. **Remove the front panel.**
Tilt the washer back and slide blocks under the front legs for easier access to the screws. Remove the screws and lift off the front panel.

1

FILTER

2

2. **Twist off the filter.**
   If your washer has a filter that's separate from the drain pump, you'll see it alongside the pump. Unscrew the filter by turning it counterclockwise. Clean it out and reinstall it.

Dryer lint cleaning tips

Prevent house fires. Clean the lint from inside your clothes dryer as well as lint caught in the exhaust vent. You can complete the cleaning in about 30 minutes.

PROFESSIONAL COST: $100

YOUR COST: $15

SAVINGS: $85

COMPLEXITY
Simple

TOOLS
4-in-1 screwdriver

MATERIALS
Dryer brush
Shop vacuum or vacuum cleaner

CAUTION:
Consult your manual for instructions on accessing the heating element or cabinet interior.

1. To clean the exhaust duct, shut off the gas and unplug the dryer, then pull the dryer away from the wall and disconnect the duct from the dryer. Use a brush and a vacuum to remove the lint in the duct. If you have a flexible duct (especially the plastic type!), replace it with rigid metal duct.

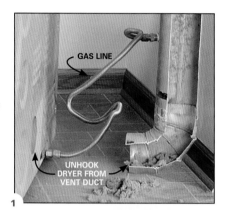

GAS LINE

UNHOOK DRYER FROM VENT DUCT

1

2. To clean inside the dryer, unplug it and turn off the gas, then open either the top or the front. (The procedure is the same for gas and electric dryers.) For dryers with a top lint filter and a solid front panel, remove the lint filter and take out the two screws on the side of the filter opening and lift it up to release it from the catches at the corners.

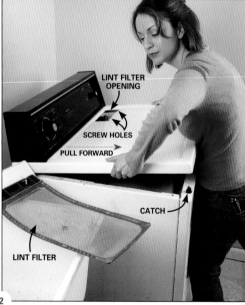

LINT FILTER OPENING

SCREW HOLES

PULL FORWARD

CATCH

LINT FILTER

2

3. Disconnect the door-switch wires in the front corner, remove the two front screws then tip the front forward and lift it clear of the bottom catches and the drum. The drum will tip as the panel drops, but this won't damage anything. Just hold it up while you clean.

4. Brush out the lint inside the lint filter opening and vacuum all around the drum. Clean thoroughly around the heating element, but work gently around wires and mechanical parts. Use a long brush to clean the vent, then vacuum it from the top and back

5. Finally, reassemble the dryer. Put the front into the drum and lift, then drop the front into the catches near the bottom while holding it tight against the sides. Reattach the front screws and wires, then set the top back down.

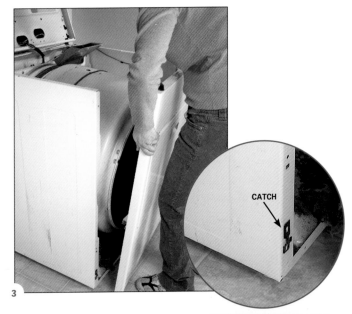

CATCH

3

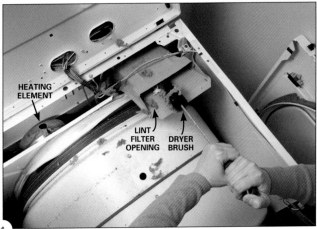

HEATING ELEMENT

LINT FILTER OPENING

DRYER BRUSH

4

pro tips!

➤ Built-up lint inside dryer cabinets causes more than 15,000 fires every year. Lint escapes through tiny gaps around the edges of the dryer drum and falls into the cabinet, especially when the exhaust vent or vent cap is clogged and airflow is restricted. The lint can get ignited by electric heating elements, gas burners or even a spark from the motor, and the flames then travel through the lint-lined exhaust vent. To make sure this doesn't happen in your house, check the exhaust vent and the inside of the cabinet frequently.

Cleaning technique if your dryer has a front access panel

1. Release the metal catches (or remove screws).

   Slide a screwdriver into the gap at the top of the bottom panel at the two catches to release the panel.

2. Vacuum out the lint. Vacuum around motor, the vent and the inside of the dryer. Clean carefully around wires and small parts to avoid breaking them.

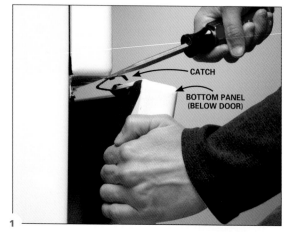

CATCH

BOTTOM PANEL (BELOW DOOR)

1

CAUTION:
Clean thoroughly around the heating element, but work gently around wires and mechanical parts.

MOTOR

HEATING ELEMENT

VENT

DRYER BRUSH

2

pro tips!

Clothes damp after a normal cycle— try these quick fixes.

➤ **Check your dryer setting.** If your clothes are damp after a normal cycle check the dryer setting—make sure it's not on "fluff air," a non-heat setting.

➤ **Clean your dryer filter.** Another common cause of poor drying is the clogged lint filter. The filter may look clean, but it may actually be covered by a nearly invisible film caused by dryer sheets. This film reduces airflow and forces the thermostat to shut off the heat before your clothes are dry. Pull out the filter and scrub it in hot water with a little laundry detergent and a stiff kitchen brush.

➤ **Also check the ouside dryer vent for any lint that may have built up there.** The louver door-style vent covers are notorious for lint buildup, which traps heat and turns the heat off in the dryer. Pull the cover completely off to get to these clogs.

PROFESSIONAL
COST: $30

YOUR COST: $5

SAVINGS: $25

COMPLEXITY
Simple

TOOLS
Flat-blade
  screwdriver

MATERIALS
Replacement belt

How to replace a vacuum cleaner belt

When your vacuum starts to lose cleaning power, requiring multiple passes to get an area clean, or the self-propulsion loses its zip, chances are you need to change the vacuum agitator belt. After only a few months of use, most vacuum belts stretch out enough to slip, causing the agitator to spin more slowly.

The good news is you can do it yourself in about 15 minutes with two screwdrivers.

1. **Remove cover screws.**
Unplug the vacuum and turn it over, exposing the underside. Back out the casing screws that secure the bottom cover. Release the attachment clips with a flat-blade screwdriver and lift off the cover.

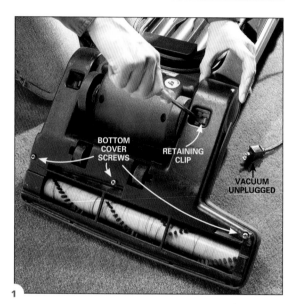

BOTTOM COVER SCREWS

RETAINING CLIP

VACUUM UNPLUGGED

1

pro tips!

➤ Replacing the belt is quick and inexpensive. New belts are available from a vacuum parts supplier (check online for a store in your area). Belts come in numerous brands and sizes, so bring the old one to the store for a guaranteed match.

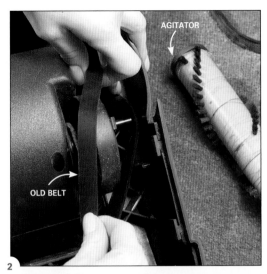

2. **Remove the belt.**
   Pry out the agitator with a flat-blade screwdriver. Slide the old belt off the agitator pulley and motor drive shaft and slide the new belt on the motor drive shaft.

3. **Seat the agitator.**
   Slide the new belt onto the agitator. Replace the agitator, making sure the end caps are properly seated.

4. Once the new belt's on and the agitator's back in place, turn the agitator by hand to make sure the belt spins smoothly, without rubbing or binding. Reassemble the bottom cover and test-run the machine.

PROFESSIONAL
COST: $30

YOUR COST: $0

SAVINGS: $30

COMPLEXITY
Simple

TOOLS
Shop vacuum
Broom handle

MATERIALS
Wire coat hanger or
  stiff electrical wire

Vacuum not picking up dirt— clean out clogs

If your vacuum cleaner isn't picking up dirt, and cleaning or replacing the filter or the bag doesn't help, you probably have a clog.

If the attachment hose has no suction, either it or the hose suction port is clogged. Try to unclog using these methods.

1. **Shop vacuum technique.** Use a shop vacuum to suck clogs out of the suction port or hose.

2. **Broom handle technique.** Shove stubborn clogs through the hose with a broom handle.

3. **Bent wire technique for the hose suction port.** If the machine isn't picking up dirt and the brushes are turning, most likely the suction port at the base of the machine is plugged. Remove the cover on the underside of the machine to access the port. Bend a little barb on the end of a coat hanger or stiff electrical wire and use it to hook the clog to pull it free.

1

2

HOSE
SUCTION
PORT

3

AC won't come on? Check the fuse

If you turn your central air conditioner on, off and then on again in rapid order, chances are you'll blow a fuse or shut off a circuit breaker or the air conditioner simply won't respond. Be patient and give the air conditioner thermostat about five minutes to reset. If it still won't come on, you may have blown a fuse.

PROFESSIONAL
COST: $150

YOUR COST: $5

SAVINGS: $145

COMPLEXITY
Simple

MATERIALS
Cartridge fuses
(if required)

FUSE
BLOCK

AIR CONDITIONER
SHUTOFF BOX

CONDENSING UNIT
(INCLUDES
COMPRESSOR)

RUUD

1

1. Locate the special fuse block near the outside unit. Pull out the block and take the whole thing to the hardware store. A salesperson can test the cartridge fuses and tell you if you need to replace them.

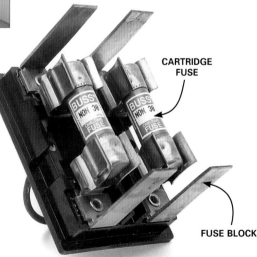

CARTRIDGE
FUSE

BUSS
NON 30

BUSS
NON 30

FUSE BLOCK

Chapter 5
Windows and Doors

PROFESSIONAL
COST: $50

YOUR COST: $0

SAVINGS: $50

COMPLEXITY
Simple

TOOLS
Flathead screwdriver
Scissors

Shorten horizontal blinds

Horizontal blind slats that hang below the windowsill are not only unsightly but also a strangulation hazard for young children. Most dangerous are the pull cords. Shortening the blinds to the proper height will raise the pull cords and make your home a safer place.

The bottom rail runs through the ladder cords, and the pull cords are knotted below the rail on each end. Photo 1 shows how to disassemble the cords from the bottom rail. If the pull cords still hang low when you're finished, install a cleat to store them higher, out of kids' reach.

1. Pry the plugs out of the bottom rail with a flathead screwdriver. Set the plugs aside for reuse later. If the pull cords are threaded through the plugs, cut them off close to the plug. If the pull cords are knotted inside the bottom rail, cut them above the rail to free it. Slide the rail out from the ladder cords and set it aside.

PLUG

BOTTOM RAIL

1

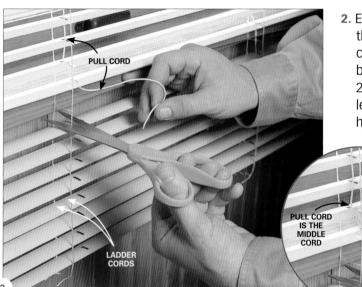

2. Extract the pull cord from the center of the ladder cords, hold it away and cut both ladder cords about 2 in. longer than the final length to make sure you have enough length to insert the strings into the holes on the bottom rail. Allow the excess slats to drop away.

PULL CORD

PULL CORD IS THE MIDDLE CORD

LADDER CORDS

CUT LADDER CORDS

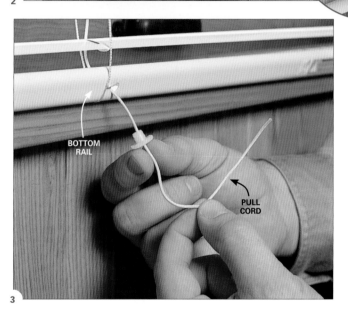

BOTTOM RAIL

PULL CORD

3. Slide the bottom rail back between the ladder cords. String the pull cords through the bottom rail and knot the ends. Make sure that the pull cords are even and that the bottom rail hangs straight. You may have to adjust the position of the knot to achieve the desired length to your blinds. Do not try to adjust the length with the pull cord. Tuck loose ends into the holes and replace the plugs.

Replace a window screen

PROFESSIONAL
COST: $50

YOUR COST: $10

SAVINGS: $40

COMPLEXITY
Simple

TOOLS
Awl or
 4-in-1 screwdriver
Drill
Scissors
Spline roller
Utility knife

MATERIALS
Screen
Spline
Wood stop block

Window screens can get punctured or torn, but as long as the frame is in good shape repairs are easy and can be done in a few minutes. Here's how to make your screen window look good as new.

Know the size of your window when you go to the home center. It will sell pre-measured rolls to fit nearly any opening size.

1. Pry out the old spline with an awl or a narrow-tipped screwdriver. Throw it away—spline gets hard and brittle as it ages and shouldn't be reused. Remove the old screen.

2. Secure the frame by placing wooden blocks along the inside of the two longest sides of the frame and secure them to the work surface. The blocks keep the frame from bowing inward when you install the new screen material.

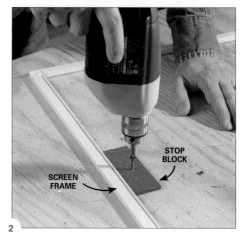

1

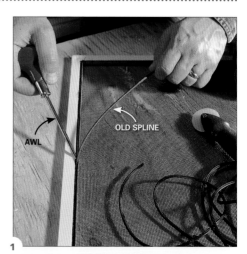

2

pro tips!

➤ The most popular replacement screen material is fiberglass, the type shown here. Its flexibility makes it the easiest to use—if you make a mistake, you can take it out of the frame and try again. Aluminum screen is sturdier, but you only get one chance. The grooves you've made with the screen rolling tool are there to stay. A third type of screen material that's popular is sun-shading fabric. It blocks more sun, which means less load on your air-conditioning system and less fading of your carpet, draperies and furniture. It's also stronger than fiberglass and aluminum screening, so it's great for pet owners.

All three materials come in gray or black to match your other window screens. You can also get shiny aluminum as well as sun-shading fabrics in bronze and brown tones.

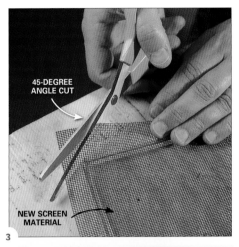

45-DEGREE ANGLE CUT

NEW SCREEN MATERIAL

3

SCREEN ROLLING TOOL

CONCAVE ROLLER

NEW SPLINE

4

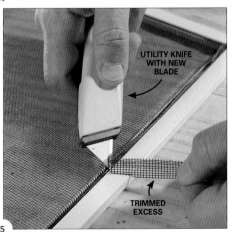

UTILITY KNIFE WITH NEW BLADE

TRIMMED EXCESS

5

3. Position the new screen. Lay the new screen material over the frame. It should overlap the frame about an inch. Cut each corner at a 45-degree angle just slightly beyond the spline groove. The cuts keep the screen from bunching in the corners.

4. Push the new screen in. Begin installing the new spline at a corner. Use the screen rolling tool with the concave wheel to push the spline and screen material into the groove. Continue around the frame, stretching the screen as you go. If wrinkles or bulges appear, remove the spline and reroll. Small wrinkles should tighten up as you get back to the starting corner. When all four splines are in place, roll them again, this time with the convex wheel.

5. Trim the excess screen material using a utility knife with a new sharp blade. A dull blade will pull the material, not cut it. Cut with the blade on top of the spline and pointed toward the outside of the frame.

CAUTION: If your screen frame is taller than 36 in., it should have a center support to keep it from bowing in once the material is in place. Newer screens usually come with this support. If your long screens don't have a support, you can make one out of aluminum frame stock. It's located near the screening supplies in most stores. The aluminum stock can be cut with a tin snips and trimmed to fit.

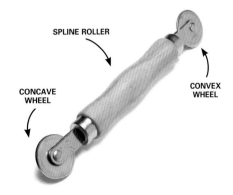

SPLINE ROLLER

CONCAVE WHEEL

CONVEX WHEEL

Replace a casement window crank operator

Don't replace your casement window if it won't open or shut completely. You can usually replace a bad crank operator in an hour, and have it working smoothly again; a bargain if the overall condition of the window is still good.

Your operator may vary slightly from the one we show. However, the replacement process is similar.

1. Inspect the old crank for wear or damage. Worn and missing splines on the crank stud, stripped or broken gears, and worn-out crank arms mean you have to replace the entire crank operator.

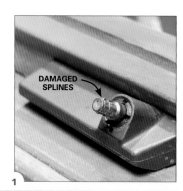

DAMAGED SPLINES

1

2. Disconnect the crank arm from the guide track. Crank the window open until the plastic guide bushing aligns with the guide track notch. Press down on the arm to free the bushing from the track, and then push out the window until the bushing clears the track. (Use a locking pliers for a crank handle and push out on the window to help it open). If the operator also contains a split arm operator, unhook that too.

PLASTIC GUIDE BUSHING

GUIDE TRACK NOTCH

ARM

2

pro tips!

➤ You don't need the make, model or serial number of the crank operator. You just need a picture. Snap a digital photo, email it to a hardware supply company and the company will sell you a new one. Or mail the company a print photo. You can also look at online catalogs to find an operator that matches yours.

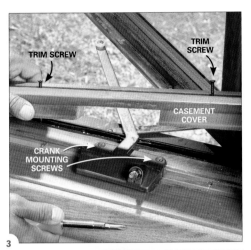

TRIM SCREW

TRIM SCREW

CASEMENT COVER

CRANK MOUNTING SCREWS

3

4

5

3. Unscrew the trim mounting screws inside the screen track. Remove the casement cover off the window jamb and access the crank innards. If there aren't any trim screws, the casement cover is probably nailed or stapled in place. Slide a stiff putty knife between the window jamb and casement cover. Carefully pry up the casing so you don't damage the wood parts. Remove all crank mounting screws and lift off the crank. Replace rusted or bent trim screws. Close the window and lock it until the new crank arrives.

4. Compare the new operator with the old to make sure they match.

5. Install the new crank. Line up the new crank with the old holes. The old screw holes are often stripped. If so, stick a toothpick or two in them as filler and drive the screws. Then reattach the crank arm and casement cover.

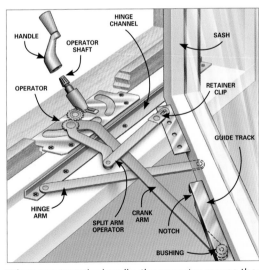

HINGE CHANNEL

HANDLE

OPERATOR SHAFT

SASH

OPERATOR

RETAINER CLIP

GUIDE TRACK

HINGE ARM

SPLIT ARM OPERATOR

CRANK ARM

NOTCH

BUSHING

When you turn the handle, the operator moves the crank arm and the split arm operator. The split arm operator then opens the window sash. Casement window operators come in several styles.

Stop drafts around windows and doors

If your windows or doors are a source of chilly drafts all winter long, the problem could be worn-out seals, weather stripping or thresholds. Then again, sloppy installation might be to blame. When cold weather arrives, hold the back of your hand near the edges of windows or doors to track down the source of leaks. If you feel cold air flowing out from behind the trim, chances are the spaces around the window and door jambs weren't properly sealed.

Plugging these leaks is a time-consuming job: You have to pull off the interior trim, seal around the jambs and then reinstall the trim. But if your doors and windows are otherwise fairly airtight, the payoff can be big, too. Stopping drafts not only makes your home more comfortable but also cuts energy bills (air leaks are a major source of heat loss in most homes).

1. First investigate: Remove one piece of trim from a window or a door. To prevent chipping or tearing paint, slice through paint where the trim meets the wall and jamb. Put a new blade in your utility knife and make several passes over heavy paint buildup.

1

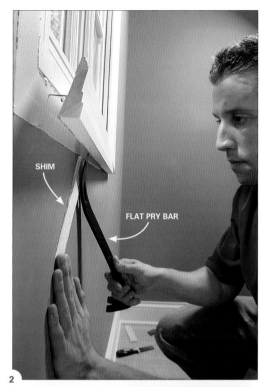

SHIM

FLAT PRY BAR

2

NIPPERS

4

2. Slip a stiff putty knife under the trim and lift it enough to insert a flat pry bar. Don't simply force up one end of the piece. Instead, work along the length of the piece, moving your pry bar and lifting the trim off gradually. Protect walls with a shim or a scrap of wood as you gradually work the trim away from the wall.

   At mitered corners, watch for nails driven through the joint. To prevent these nails from splitting mitered ends, pry up both mitered pieces together. Then pull them apart.

3. With one piece removed, examine the space between the jamb and the wall framing. If the drywall covers the space, trim it back with a utility knife. If you see only a few loose wads of fiberglass insulation or no insulation at all between the jamb and framing, it's likely that all your windows and doors are poorly sealed and need sealant.
   Continue to remove the remaining trim.

4. Pull nails out through the back side of trim with nippers or pliers to avoid damaging the face of the trim. Also write the location of each piece of trim on the back side.

5. Fill gaps with foam sealant. Pull insulation from between the jamb and the wall framing. Seal the gap around the jamb with foam sealant. Some sealants will push jambs inward as they expand, so be sure to use one that's intended for windows and doors (check the label). We chose DAP Tex Plus because it's easy to clean up with a damp rag. Most expanding foams are nearly impossible to clean up before they harden.

   Let the foam harden and trim off any excess foam with a knife before you reinstall the trim.

6. Position each piece exactly as it was originally and tack each one up with only two nails. Ridges in the wall paint can help you align each piece perfectly. With only a couple of nails in each piece, you can make small adjustments by holding a block against the trim and tapping it with a hammer. Then add more nails. If your trim has a clear finish, fill the nail holes with a matching colored filler such as Color Putty or DAP Finishing Putty. With painted trim, it's best to fill the holes with spackle and repaint.

FOAM SEALANT   WALL FRAMING

JAMB

5

6

Repairing a loose door handle

Over time, door handles loosen and become difficult to turn and unlatch. Most door hardware made today uses exposed screws, accessible from the "room side" of the door, to connect the two halves of the handle to each side of the door. But some current brands (and most older door hardware) use hidden chassis screws, a setup that requires you to take the doorknob and rose (cover plate) apart to tighten the screws. It only takes a minute to pop off the cover plate.

Our door hardware is fairly typical, but you may have something other than a button to release the knob. Also, some door roses unscrew from the chassis by hand (turn them counterclockwise) rather than snap onto it.

PROFESSIONAL COST: $50

YOUR COST: $0

SAVINGS: $50

COMPLEXITY
Simple

TOOLS
4-in-1 screwdriver
Awl if required

1. Remove the inside doorknob by locating the button (like our model), metal tab or wire clip on the side of the knob that acts as a release. Using an awl or small screwdriver, push the button in all the way—and at the same time—pull off the handle. Remove the door rose by inserting a small screwdriver into the small notch in the rose and twisting the tool to pop it off. Be careful so you don't chip any door paint.

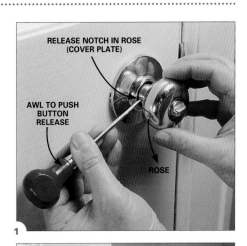

RELEASE NOTCH IN ROSE (COVER PLATE)

AWL TO PUSH BUTTON RELEASE

ROSE

1

2. Tighten the door hardware by opening the door, squeezing both sides of the assembly together and tightening the two screws on the chassis. To reassemble, snap the rose back on the chassis, depress the release button and slide the knob back on until the button pops through the hole.

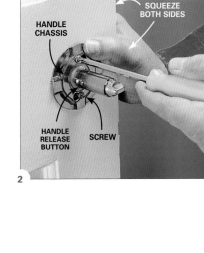

HANDLE CHASSIS

SQUEEZE BOTH SIDES

HANDLE RELEASE BUTTON   SCREW

2

PROFESSIONAL
COST: $50

YOUR COST: $0

SAVINGS: $50

COMPLEXITY
Simple

TOOLS
Drill/driver, cordless

MATERIALS
3-in. yellow
   dichromate (zinc-
   plated) screws

Door sticking—fix hinge screws

One day the door closes smoothly; the next day it's sticking. And the sticking grows worse as the weeks pass. It's a common old house problem, but it can happen anywhere.

The problem is loose hinges. The solution is simple and foolproof—bigger screws! You'll have that sticking door working like a charm in no time.

1. The screws holding the top hinges carry most of the weight of the door and are almost always the first to pull out, especially after they've been repeatedly tightened over the years. The best way to beef them up is to replace the standard 3/4-in. hinge screws with at least two 3-in. screws that go through the jambs and solidly anchor into the framing. If

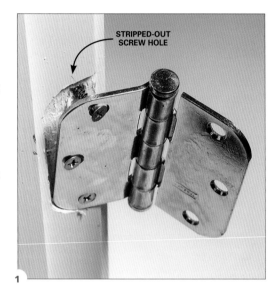

STRIPPED-OUT
SCREW HOLE

1

the door has a large hinge with four screw holes, just drive 3-in. screws straight through the two holes toward the center of the door. However, if the hinge has only three holes, add a 3-in. screw through the middle hole and redrill the top screw hole at a slight angle so the screw hits solid wood.

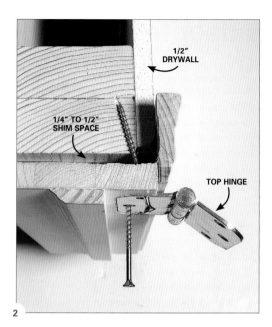

1/2" DRYWALL

1/4" TO 1/2" SHIM SPACE

TOP HINGE

2

pro tips!

➤ When drilling, brace yourself against the latch-side jamb and push hard to avoid stripping the screwhead.

2. Start the drill bit at a sharp angle so the bit doesn't follow the old screw hole. As soon as you feel a fresh hole starting, tip the drill bit back to an angle that will hit the stud—the angle shown here should work for most doors. If the bit or screw feels like it's sliding off to the side between the drywall and wood, redrill at a sharper angle. Replace short hinge screws with long screws when the screw holes no longer hold. Angle the long screws toward the studs to make sure they catch.

3. Screw the hinge back in with yellow dichromate (zinc-plated) screws—the color and head size of these rust-resistant drywall screws are a good match for standard brass hinge screws. If the door doesn't shut properly after all the screws are driven in, they may have been driven in too far, pulling the door frame out of plumb. Just back the screws out a few turns.

COMPLEXITY
Simple

TOOLS
Pliers
Hammer

MATERIALS
Shim
Large nail
Wood scraps

How to stop a door from swinging open

If you have a door that swings all the way open every time you leave it slightly ajar, the door frame isn't plumb. But you don't need to hire someone to take the door down and go through the hassle of disassembling everything just to adjust the frame. Instead, try this much simpler fix.

Grab a hammer, a few scraps of wood, a large nail and a shim. Take them into the room and close the door. Reinsert the pin and check the results. If the door still won't stay open, do the same with the lower hinge.

1. Stick the shim loosely between the door and the jamb to hold the door in position when you drive out the upper hinge pin. Knock out the upper hinge pin by tapping a nail up from underneath with a hammer. Once the pin is loose, pull it out.

    Lift up on the door handle to relieve pressure if the pin binds. Keep the door closed and work on one hinge at a time.

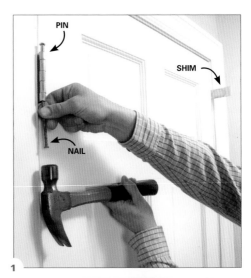

2. Bend the pin slightly. Hold the hinge pin with pliers. Hit the pin with a hammer. The bent pin should keep the door from swinging open on its own. Reinsert the pin and check the results. If the door still won't stay open, do the same with the lower hinge.

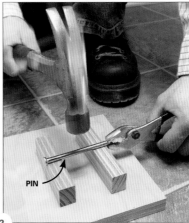

How to make perfect-closing screen doors

We'll show you how to adjust a screen door so it closes perfectly. By simply turning a screw, you can fix the door so it won't slam shut or be hard to pull closed. If you can use a screwdriver, you can fix this problem.

PROFESSIONAL
COST: $50

YOUR COST: $0

SAVINGS: $50

COMPLEXITY
Simple

TOOLS
4-in-1 screwdriver
Snap-on locking
pliers if required

1. Lock the door open with the hold-open washer to release the tension on the pin. Remove the pin. Move the connecting pin to the inner hole to make the door close harder. For a softer close, use the outer hole.

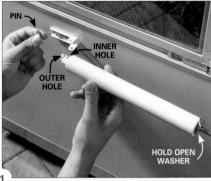

2. If moving the pin makes matters worse, return it to its original position and try the adjustment screw. Turn it clockwise for a softer close, counterclockwise for harder. Make a quarter turn, test the door and continue making quarter turns until the door closes just right. If your door has two closers, treat them exactly alike. Adjust both screws equally and make sure their pins are in the same position.

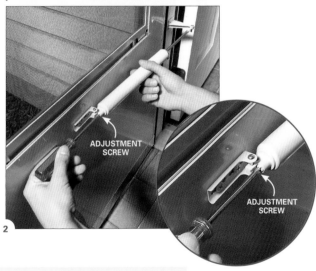

pro tips!

➤ If your hold-open washer won't work, open the door and snap on locking pliers (such as a Vise-Grip pliers) onto the closer shaft to hold the door open.
To repair the washer, slip it off the shaft, put it in a vise and make a sharper bend in it using a hammer or take the entire closer to a hardware store and find a similar replacement. Some closers mount a little differently from the one we show. For example, you may find that the door bracket, rather than the closer, has two pinholes.

PROFESSIONAL
COST: $50

YOUR COST: $20

SAVINGS: $30

COMPLEXITY
Simple

TOOLS
4-in-1 screwdriver
Measuring tape
Cordless drill
Drill bit set

MATERIALS
Replacement storm-
door handle and
latch
Pencil

Replace a broken screen- or storm-door handle

Trade in the broken, shabby push-button handle on your screen- or storm-door for a shiny new easy-opening lever handle. Replacement handles will fit most aluminum, steel and some wood doors. The handles are available at hardware stores and home centers. You can swap out the handle in about ten minutes.

1. Remove the old storm-door handle by unscrewing the two screws that hold the two halves together. Pull the interior and exterior handles apart and remove the center spindle. Discard the old handle.

BROKEN HANDLE

1

pro tips!

➤ If at first glance it appeared that the new handle would fit in the old holes, but a closer look at the instructions revealed the handle had to be shifted slightly away from the edge of the door, rather than attempt to enlarge the holes and risk a sloppy fit, move the handle down slightly and drill new holes. Manufacturers generally anticipated this problem and provided a cover plate to conceal the old holes on the inside of the door.

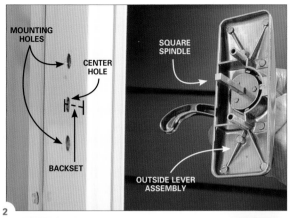

MOUNTING HOLES

CENTER HOLE

BACKSET

SQUARE SPINDLE

OUTSIDE LEVER ASSEMBLY

2

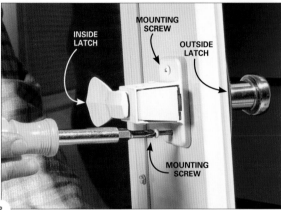

INSIDE LATCH

MOUNTING SCREW

OUTSIDE LATCH

MOUNTING SCREW

3

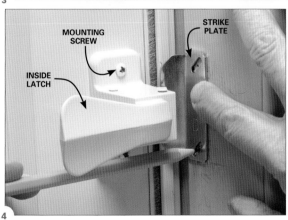

MOUNTING SCREW

STRIKE PLATE

INSIDE LATCH

4

2. You'll see three vertically spaced mounting holes in the screen door (wood doors may require different hardware). Measure the distance from the edge of the door to the center of one of these holes. This distance is called the backset. Buy a new handle with the same backset, or use the manufacturer's enclosed drilling template to relocate the 5/16-in. mounting screw holes. Assemble the new door handle according to the instructions on the packaging and slide the spindle through the center hole.

3. Slide the interior latch over the protruding spindle and screw the two halves together with the machine screws provided. Start the screws by hand to make sure the threads are aligned before tightening them with a screwdriver.

4. Hold the new strike plate in place with the door closed (have a helper push it tight from the outside). Mark the center of the mounting slots for maximum adjustability. Drill 3/32-in. pilot holes in the door jamb and screw down the new strike plate to the door frame. (Use the plastic shims provided to shim the plate if necessary. Adjust the strike plate until the door latches firmly, then tighten the screws.)

PROFESSIONAL
COST: $150

YOUR COST: $46

SAVINGS: $104

COMPLEXITY
Moderate

TOOLS
Hammer
Wood chisel
Needle-nose pliers
Tape measure
Caulk gun
4-in-1 screwdriver
Nail set
Stapler
Rubber mallet
Utility knife

MATERIALS
1-in. brad nails
Weather stripping
Door sweep
Caulk
1/2-in staples if
  required

How to stop door drafts around entry doors

With heating costs going through the roof, here's an easy way to keep heat from slipping out your doors, too. Take 30 minutes and replace the weather stripping and door sweeps around your steel entry doors. Plan to do this project on a warm day since you'll have to remove the doors. Steel doors use a compression-style strip for the hinge side and a magnetic one for the knob side and the top. But look at the door and confirm the style of weather stripping on all three sides and the type of door sweep before you head to the store. You'll find replacement weather stripping in a variety of lengths and colors at home centers and hardware stores.

1. To remove the door, close it and use a hammer and a pin punch or a thin nail to tap out the door hinge pins. Turn the knob, open the door slightly and lift it off the hinges.

2. Remove old weather stripping. Rip out the old, damaged weather stripping, pulling it through the brads that hold it in. Leave them in place after removing the old weather stripping or you'll damage the doorjamb.

3. Cut the brads or push them all the way back into the groove with an old chisel.

WEATHER STRIP GROOVE

EXISTING BRAD

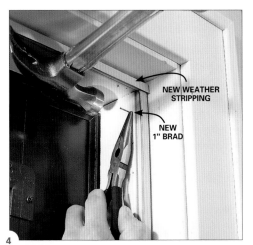

NEW WEATHER STRIPPING

NEW 1" BRAD

4

4. Cut the new weather stripping to length and reinstall it. Press the new magnetic weather stripping firmly into the groove on the knob side and top of the door frame and do the same with the compression strip along the hinge side. To ensure that the strips won't pull out, pin them with a few 1-in. brads positioned near the old one, especially in the magnetic strips.

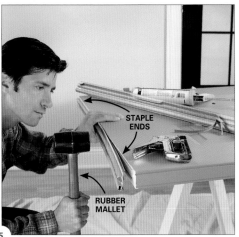

STAPLE ENDS

RUBBER MALLET

5

5. Attach new sweep. Pry or slide out the old sweep. Run a bead of caulk along the bottom edge of the door, tap the sweep into place and then staple it at the ends with 1/2-in. staples or the fasteners provided with the sweep.

ADJUSTMENT SCREW

NO. 3 SCREWDRIVER

6

6. Adjust the door threshold with a No. 3 Phillips screwdriver. Adjust all four screws until the door opens and closes without too much drag and any drafts have been eliminated (look for light between the sweep and the threshold with the door closed). Turn the screws clockwise to lower the threshold and counterclockwise to raise it.

PROFESSIONAL
COST: $50

YOUR COST: $0

SAVINGS: $50

COMPLEXITY
Simple

TOOLS
4-in-1 screwdriver

MATERIALS
Silicone spray
 lubricant
Replacement rollers

Adust a dragging shower door

If the sliding doors on your shower or bathtub don't glide smoothly, repair them soon. A door that drags on the lower track will eventually do permanent damage to both the door and the track. A dragging roller at the top of the door will wear and require replacement.

First, make sure the rollers on both doors are riding on the tracks inside the upper rail. Sometimes, one roller falls out of the track and the bottom edge of the door skids along the lower rail. In that case, you only have to lift the door and guide the roller back onto the track.

If an off-track roller isn't the problem, you'll have to remove the doors to adjust and possibly replace the rollers. Many doors have a small plastic guide at the middle of the lower rail. To remove this type of guide, just remove a single screw. Others have a guide rail screwed to the door as shown.

1. Unscrew the guide at the lower edge of the sliding door. Protect the shower or tub from scratches with a drop cloth.

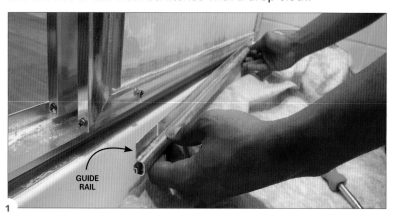

GUIDE
RAIL

1

pro tips!

➤ Most home centers and some hardware stores carry replacements. Take an old roller with you to find a match. In many cases, you can use a replacement that's slightly larger or smaller than the original. But be sure the original and replacement edges match—either rounded or flat (see photo of roller types). If you can't find rollers locally, type "shower door parts" into any online search engine to find a supplier.

UPPER RAIL

2. Lift the door out of its track inside the upper rail. Tilt each door in or out to remove it. Wipe both tracks clean. Then make sure the rollers turn easily. If not, apply a little silicone spray lubricant. Some lubricants can harm plastic, so check the label. If the lubricant doesn't do the trick, replace the rollers.

3. Screw the new rollers into place and rehang the doors. Raise or lower each door by repositioning the roller in its slanted slot. Loosen the screw to move the roller. You'll probably have to remove the doors once or twice to adjust the rollers for smooth operation.

ROUND EDGE

FLAT EDGE

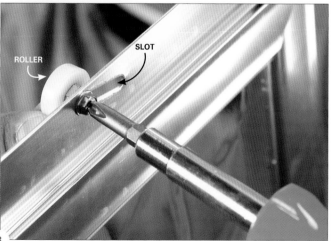

ROLLER

SLOT

Chapter 6
Walls and Floors

Patch a drywall hole fast

The traditional method of repairing holes in walls is to square the hole, put wood backing behind it, cut and screw on a drywall patch, and then tape the edges. Aluminum patches, available at home centers and paint and hardware stores, give the same results with much less work. The patches, which come in various sizes, are stiff enough to span holes and thin enough to disappear after taping and painting.

Select a patch large enough to overlap the hole on all sides by an inch. Patches can be cut or overlapped as needed.

PROFESSIONAL
COST: $100

YOUR COST: $10

SAVINGS: $90

COMPLEXITY
Simple

TOOLS
Mud pan
12-in. wide taping
  knife
Sanding sponge,
  120-grit

MATERIALS
Dust mask
Aluminum patch
Pre-mixed joint
  compound
Primer
Paint

CAUTION:
When working with
drywall it is always
recommended to
wear a dust mask.

1. Clean off broken edges and tears around the hole. Then cover the hole entirely with the patch, sticky side toward the wall.

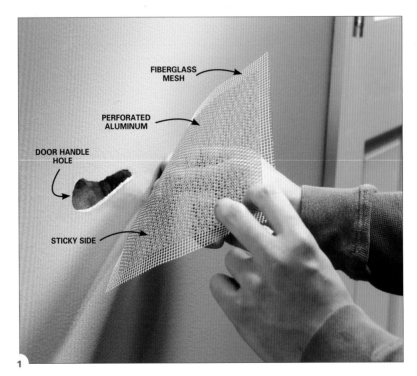

FIBERGLASS MESH

PERFORATED ALUMINUM

DOOR HANDLE HOLE

STICKY SIDE

1

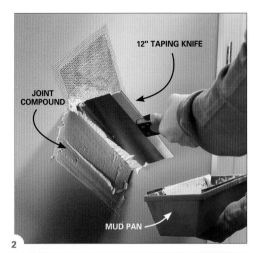

JOINT COMPOUND

12" TAPING KNIFE

MUD PAN

2

3

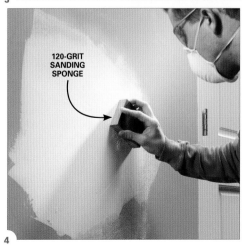

120-GRIT SANDING SPONGE

4

2. Prepare joint compound per manufacturer's instructions. Spread the first coat of joint compound over the patch with a wide taping knife, flat enough to see the outline of the mesh through it. Let it dry overnight.

3. When it's dry, apply a wider second coat and then feather out the compound on all sides to make the patch blend in. Then apply a final, third coat after the second coat dries. Spread the compound in thin coats extending 8 to 12 in. beyond the patch in all directions.

4. After final coat has dried, sand the patched area with a sanding sponge until it feels smooth and even. Prime and then paint.

Repair a drywall crack

PROFESSIONAL COST: $100

YOUR COST: $10

SAVINGS: $90

COMPLEXITY
Simple

TOOLS
Mud pan
Painters tape
Utility knife
6-in. taping knife
12-in. taping knife
Sanding sponge,
 120-grit

MATERIALS
Dust mask
Paper drywall tape
Pre-mixed joint
 compound

CAUTION:
When working with drywall it is always recommended to wear a dust mask.

Eventually even the best-built houses develop a few cracks due to settling, usually around doors and windows. Learn how to fix them the right way, so they don't come back.

Whether your walls are made of plaster or drywall, you can repair the cracks in two steps over a day or two—and get the area ready to sand and paint. Use paper tape; it's stronger than fiberglass tape for wall repairs.

....

1. Cut a V-notch through the full length of the crack, 1/8 to 1/4 in. deep, removing all loose wall material. Protect woodwork with painters tape.

PAINTERS TAPE TO PROTECT WOOD

1

pro tips!

➤ For cracks more than 1/4 in. deep, clean out the loose material and use a quick-setting crack filler like Durabond to build up the area level with the wall. Then use the steps shown in photos 2 and 3 to fix.

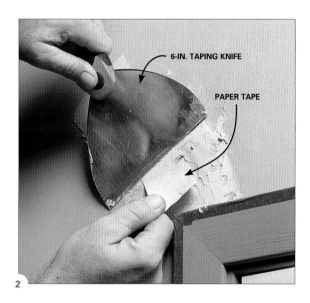

6-IN. TAPING KNIFE

PAPER TAPE

2

12-IN. TAPING KNIFE

3

2. Embed paper tape in joint compound using a 6-in. taping knife. To avoid trapping air bubbles under the tape, moisten the paper tape with water, lay it over the crack and squeeze excess compound and air from underneath with the blade. Apply an additional thin layer of compound and feather it off 2 in. on both sides of the tape. Let dry.

3. Apply a second (and third, if necessary) coat of compound, smoothing it out 6 to 7 in. on both sides of the joint. Smooth the compound to a thin, even coat using long, continuous strokes with a 12-in. taping blade. Allow the repair to dry thoroughly, sand it smooth (avoid exposing the tape) and paint it.

PROFESSIONAL
COST: $60

YOUR COST: $10

SAVINGS: $50

COMPLEXITY
Simple

TOOLS
Hammer
Nail set
Utility knife
4-in-1 screwdriver
6-in. taping knife
Mud pan
Sanding sponge,
  120-grit

MATERIALS
Drywall screws
Pre-mixed joint
  compound

Fix small holes and nail pops

Small holes caused by screws or hooks, wall fasteners or drywall fasteners that pop up are simple to repair, but again time-consuming because you almost always have to repaint the walls. Nail pops are common and particularly irritating, because you're likely to have more than one. But drywall screws sometimes pop up too, as a result of damp framing that dries out and shrinks during the first year or two in new construction. The good news is that you can fix all these problems yourself. You only need a few inexpensive tools and a bit of finesse. Even beginners can get good results.

1. Drive a popped nail below the surface of the drywall with a hammer and a nail set. If you have screws, dig the drywall compound from their heads with a utility knife and turn them in tight with a screwdriver.

   Then dimple the hole slightly concave with a hammer to indent any raised edges. But take care not to crush the drywall core. In addition, cut away any loose joint compound and paper tears with a sharp utility knife. This is a good technique to use with old wall fasteners as well. It's usually easier to tap them into the wall slightly rather than pull them out.

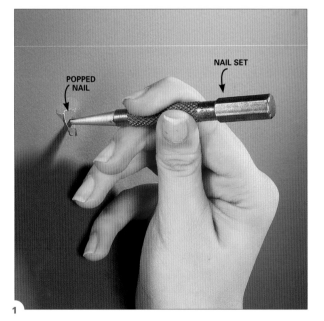

POPPED
NAIL

NAIL SET

1

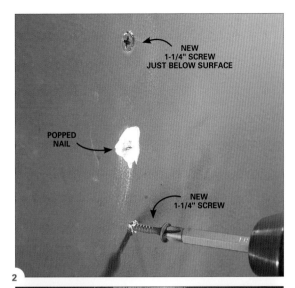

NEW
1-1/4" SCREW
JUST BELOW SURFACE

POPPED
NAIL

NEW
1-1/4" SCREW

2

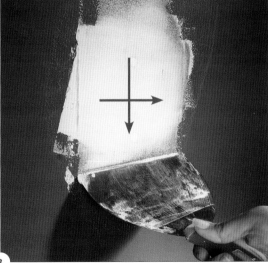

3

2. Drive drywall screws about 1-1/2 in. above and below the popped nail. Sink the screwhead just below the surface of the drywall.

3. Prepare compound with manufacturers directions. Fill the holes with joint compound, with a 6-in. taping knife, swiping first across the holes, then down in a "+" pattern. Let dry, apply a second coat. The first coat will shrink a bit, leaving a slightly smaller dent to be filled by the second coat. Scrape the excess off the surrounding wall so you don't build up a hump. Sand lightly to blend with the surrounding wall. Prime and paint.

pro tips!

➤ Be sure to prime the spot. Otherwise the topcoat will absorb into the patch and make the area look different from the surrounding paint. It is best to use a roller when priming to help raise the surface texture to match the surrounding wall.

PROFESSIONAL
COST: $70

YOUR COST: $0

SAVINGS: $70

COMPLEXITY
Simple

TOOLS
Laser level
Level
Tape measure
Hammer

MATERIALS
Paper
Painters tape
Sticky notes
Picture hanging wire
Picture hooks
Rubber bumpers

Hang pictures straight and level

Hanging a single picture is as easy as nailing a hook to the wall. But when you want to hang two or more aligned with each other, things get complicated. Here's how pros achieve perfection fast and frustration-free.

1. **Level and align.** Make paper patterns identical to the pictures, then establish a level line on the wall. An inexpensive laser level is perfect for this project, but a standard level will also work. When you've arranged the patterns perfectly, mark the top center of each with the corner of a sticky note as a reference point.

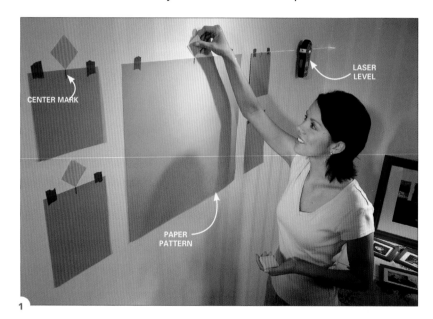

pro tips!

➤ Most experts recommend hanging a picture with its center about 60 in. from the floor, or bottom edge 6 to 8 in. above a piece of furniture. Use these heights as a starting point. Then adjust the position of the picture to your liking, and mark the top center with the corner of a sticky note.

2

2. **Find the hanger locations.** Use two hangers for each picture for extra support and to help keep the picture from tipping. Stretch the hanger wire with two fingers spaced equally distant from the edges of the picture frame. Keep the wire parallel to the top of the frame. Measure the distance between your fingertips.

3

3. **Find the distance from the top edge.** Leave one finger in place and measure from the wire to the top. Use this and the previous dimension to position the picture hangers on the wall.

4. **Transfer the hanger measurements to the wall.** Find the hanger positions by measuring down from the sticky note and to each side from the center. An inexpensive level with inches marked on it makes this much easier. Keep the hangers level.

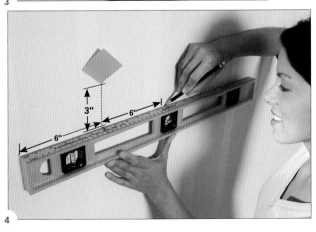

4

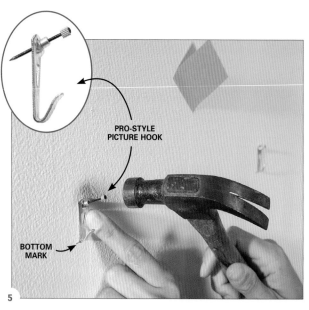

PRO-STYLE PICTURE HOOK

BOTTOM MARK

5

5. **Nail the hooks.** Then line up the bottom of the hooks with the marks and drive the picture-hanger nails through the angled guides on the hooks.

6. **Before you hang the picture.** Stick a pair of clear rubber bumpers on the back lower corners of the frame to protect the wall and help keep the picture level. You'll find these with the picture hanging supplies or in the cabinet hardware department (they're called "door bumpers").

7

7. **Hang the picture.** Slip the wire over both hooks. Slide the picture sideways across the wires until it's level. Use the same process to hang the remaining pictures.

How to remove a wall anchor without wrecking your wall

The great thing about hollow wall anchors is that they provide a cheap, fast method for attaching heavy stuff to drywall. There are at least a half dozen wall anchor devices; each works on a slightly different principle. What happens when you want to change the location of a family photo or a mirror? Some plastic, cone-shaped, expanding anchors can be pulled out from the front of the wall. But the T-nut head wall anchor shown here can't be pulled out intact, because its four expanded flanges lock up against the backside of the wall. What's the trick to remove one? Punch it through the wall which does minimal damage and simplifies wall patching.

PROFESSIONAL COST: $50

YOUR COST: $0

SAVINGS: $50

COMPLEXITY
Simple

TOOLS
Needle-nose pliers

MATERIALS
Nail
Drywall/patching compound

1. First, remove the threaded bolt that attaches your accessory to the wall anchor. Now, grab the T-nut head firmly with needle-nose pliers, then bend and pull the collar back and forth until the head snaps off. To minimize wall damage, avoid digging the nose of the pliers too wide of the collar.

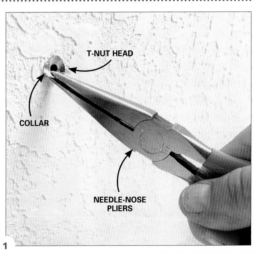

T-NUT HEAD

COLLAR

NEEDLE-NOSE PLIERS

1

2. Push the anchor body into the wall cavity with a nail. Repair the wall with patching compound and then paint the spot.

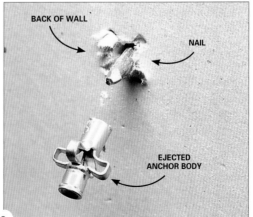

BACK OF WALL

NAIL

EJECTED ANCHOR BODY

2

How to repair damaged wallpaper

Your doorknob has slammed into the wall one too many times, and now it's punched clear through. The worst wall to repair is one covered with wallpaper. Not only must you repair the wall surface, but you've got to undertake the tricky task of installing an "invisible" wallpaper patch. Budget about two hours over two days to repair the wall. As you work, apply these tips.

1. Cut an oversized swatch of leftover wallpaper and position it over the damaged area so it extends at least 6 in. in all directions beyond the damaged area. Match the patterns. This extra space allows adequate area for feathering out joint compound around the hole repair.

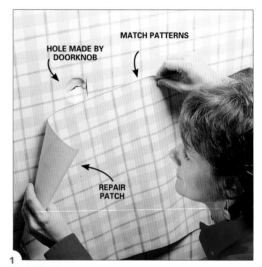

2. Cut the new patch oversize. Don't wet it or apply paste. Then tape the new paper (blue tape) directly over the existing wallpaper so the wallpaper patterns match. To establish the cutting lines, place marked pieces of tape (red tape) on the wall to mark the horizontal and vertical cutting lines. Lay a metal straightedge between these lines. When you cut the new

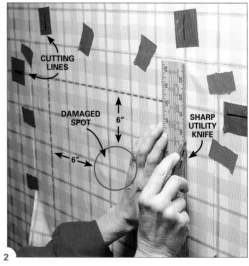

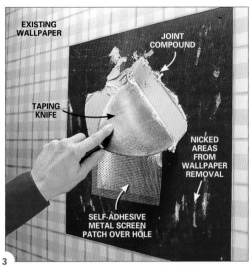

EXISTING WALLPAPER

JOINT COMPOUND

TAPING KNIFE

NICKED AREAS FROM WALLPAPER REMOVAL

SELF-ADHESIVE METAL SCREEN PATCH OVER HOLE

3

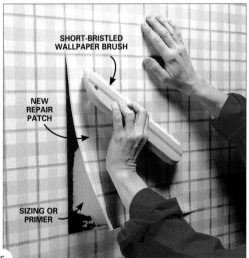

SHORT-BRISTLED WALLPAPER BRUSH

NEW REPAIR PATCH

SIZING OR PRIMER

5

patch, you'll also be cutting a hole exactly the same size out of the old wallpaper. To avoid ragged cuts, put a new blade in your knife. Double-cut through both the new patch and old wallpaper. Remove the patch and carefully scrape off the old wallpaper.

If you nick the wall surface when scraping off the old paper, fill the nicks with joint compound and sand the repairs flat.

3. Repair the wall. Apply a self-sticking metal screen patch over the hole after removing the patch and old paper. Apply two coats of joint compound in thin layers, feathering it out at the edges and sanding the repair flat. Since the hole repair will be covered by wallpaper, it doesn't have to look as perfect as a regular wall repair.

4. Before applying the patch (Photo 5), seal the repaired wall by brushing on a coat of wallpaper sizing or oil-based primer. This step ensures a tighter bond between the wallpaper patch and the wall.

5. Install the new patch. Wet the patch (if prepasted) or apply the paste, carefully matching the pattern lines between the patch and the wall (stretch the paper sparingly to fit). Smooth out any air bubbles or wrinkles with long pulling strokes using a short-bristled wallpaper brush. Work the brush from the middle out to the sides. Use a dampened sponge to remove any glue residue or fingerprints.

Fix bad wallpaper seams

Repairing loose wallpaper seams is fairly simple and it doesn't require a steamer. Just apply a seam repair adhesive. It provides a solid bond and will keep the seams from coming loose. It's available at paint stores and home centers for less than $10.

1. Squirt the adhesive directly onto the wall behind the loose seams, then press the edges back into place.

2. Use a roller or straightedge to firmly press the paper against the wall and drive out any air bubbles. Wipe away any excess adhesive with a damp sponge.

2

Straighten bubbling wallpaper

Fixing bubbles in wallpaper by cutting them with a razor knife and then the addition of a little glue can save you from costly repair! The glue applicators and adhesive are available at paint stores and home centers for less than $10.

PROFESSIONAL
COST: $100

YOUR COST: $10

SAVINGS: $90

COMPLEXITY
Simple

TOOLS
Razor knife
Glue applicator
Wallpaper smoothing tool or plastic straightedge

MATERIALS
Adhesive
Sponge

1. Cut a small slit in the bubbled area. Then insert the end of a glue applicator in the slit and squeeze in a little adhesive.

2. Wipe away excessive adhesive with a damp sponge and press the wallpaper against the wall to force out the air, using a plastic straightedge.

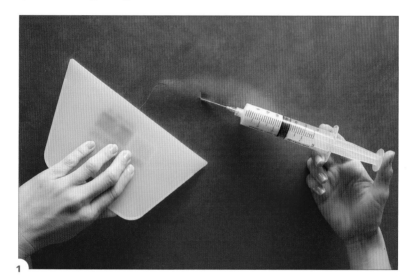

1

YOUR COST: $90

SAVINGS: $220

COMPLEXITY
Simple

TOOLS
Paint roller
Paint scraper
Putty knife
Paintbrush
Threaded wooden
 handle

MATERIALS
Bucket
Painters tape
Paint
Primer
Bucket screen
Roller sleeve
 (1/2-in. nap wool
 blend roller)

Paint walls the easy way!

These DIY painting tips will help you roll your walls quickly and smoothly—without leaving roller marks. We'll show you the tricks and techniques that painting pros use to get a perfectly painted room. All you need are some basic tools to paint fast, get great results and make clean-up a breeze. Painting is one of the least expensive ways to make over a room, so grab a roller and let's get to work.

However, even the best technique won't work with poor-quality equipment. Don't waste your money on those all-in-one throwaway roller setups when you can buy a pro setup that will last a lifetime for under $20. Start with a good roller frame, sturdy and designed to keep the roller cover from slipping off while you paint. To extend your reach and give you better control, screw a 48-in. wood handle ($3) onto the end of the roller. You could also use a threaded broom handle. You'll need a container for the paint. While most homeowners use paint trays, you'll rarely see a pro using one. That's because a 5-gallon bucket with a special bucket screen hung over the edge works a lot better.

1. Since rollers can't get tight to edges, the first painting step is to brush along the ceiling, inside corners and moldings. This "cutting in" process leaves brush marks that won't match the roller texture on the rest of the wall.

For the best-looking job, you'll want to cover as many brush marks as possible with the roller. Do this by carefully rolling up close to inside corners, moldings and the ceiling. Face the open end of the roller toward the edge and remember not to use a roller that's fully loaded with paint. With practice, you'll be able to get within an inch of the ceiling rolling vertically, and can avoid crawling up on a ladder to paint horizontally.

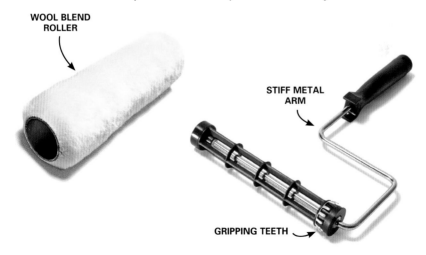

WOOL BLEND
ROLLER

STIFF METAL
ARM

GRIPPING TEETH

2. A good roller cover is the most important part of your rolling setup. Buy a 1/2-in. nap wool blend roller cover and give it a try. With proper care, this may be the last roller cover you'll ever buy.

   Wool covers do have a few drawbacks, though. They tend to shed fibers when they're first used. To minimize shedding, wrap the new roller cover with masking tape and peel it off to remove loose fibers. Repeat this a few times. Wool covers also tend to become matted down if you apply too much pressure while painting. Rolling demands a light touch. No matter what roller cover you're using, always let the paint do the work. Keep the roller cover loaded with paint and use only enough pressure to release and spread the paint. Pushing on the roller to squeeze out the last drop of paint will only cause problems.

3. Load the roller cover with paint by dipping into the paint about 1/2 in. and then rolling it against the screen. Filling a dry roller cover with paint will require five or six repetitions. After that, two or three dips are all you need. Leave the roller almost dripping with paint.

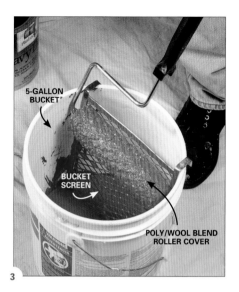

5-GALLON BUCKET

BUCKET SCREEN

POLY/WOOL BLEND ROLLER COVER

3

pro tips!

Here are a few of the advantages of a bucket and screen over a roller pan:

➤ It's easy to move the bucket without spilling.

➤ The bucket holds more paint. You won't have to frequently refill a pan.

➤ You're less likely to trip over or step in a bucket of paint.

➤ It's quicker and easier to load the roller cover with paint from a bucket.

➤ It's easy to cover a bucket with a damp cloth to prevent the paint from drying out while you're taking a lunch break.

Use an old drywall compound bucket or buy a clean new bucket. Add the bucket screen and you're ready to go.

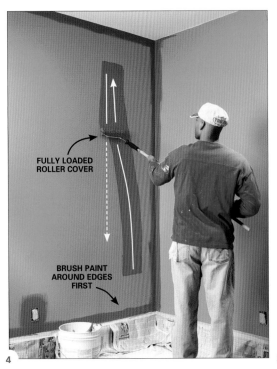

FULLY LOADED
ROLLER COVER

BRUSH PAINT
AROUND EDGES
FIRST

4

5

4. Roll paint on the wall. Lay the paint on the wall with a sweeping stroke. Start about a foot from the bottom and 6 in. from the corner and roll upward at a slight angle using light pressure. Stop a few inches from the ceiling. Now roll up and down back toward the corner to quickly spread the paint.

5. Repeat step 3. Reload the roller and repeat the process in the adjacent space, working back toward the painted area. Don't worry about uneven coverage or ridges at this point—just get the wall covered quickly. Water-based paints dry fast. If you move too slow, some areas will become sticky before you can smooth them and you'll end up with texture differences on the paint's surface.

6

6. Smooth it out. Steps 1 and 2 will give you a covered section about 4 ft. wide, but it won't look good. So go back to the beginning—without reloading the roller—and make long up-and-down strokes to even out the paint. Press lightly and overlap your strokes by 3 to 4 in. Repeat this process to cover the entire wall.

pro tips!

Ridges of paint left by the edge of the roller, or "fat edges," are a common problem. And if left to dry, they can be difficult to get rid of without heavy sanding or patching. Here are a few ways to avoid the problem.

➤ Don't submerge the roller in the paint to load it. Paint can seep inside the roller cover and leak out while you're rolling. Try to dip only the nap. Then spin it against the screen and dip again until it's loaded with paint.

➤ Don't press too hard when you're smoothing out the paint.

➤ Never start against an edge, like a corner or molding, with a full roller of paint. You'll leave a heavy buildup of paint that can't be spread out. Start about 6 in. from the edge, then unload the paint from the roller. Then work back toward the edge.

➤ Unload excess paint from the open end of the roller before you roll back over the wall to smooth it out. Do this by tilting the roller and applying a little extra pressure to the open side of the roller while rolling it up and down in the area you've just painted.

ROLLER MARKS

PAINT NOT SMOOTHED

FINISHED AREA

pro tips!

Masking tips for the perfect paint job

Masking off baseboard and other trim is a great way to get a professional-looking paint job. You'll get a crisp, clean paint line where the walls meet the trim. And the job will go quicker because you'll avoid the time-consuming "cutting in" with the paintbrush and cleaning up paint spatters from your woodwork.

Clean molding before applying painter's tape

➤ **Even the stickiest masking tape won't stay put if you apply it to a dusty, dirty surface.** You'll save yourself a lot of time and frustration if you start every masking job by cleaning the moldings or the wall to which you're applying the tape.

Pull from the roll to get the tape perfectly straight

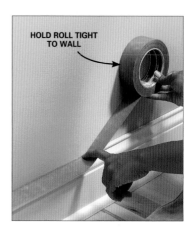

HOLD ROLL TIGHT TO WALL

➤ **One of the trickiest parts of masking is getting the tape on straight and tight against the wall.** Position the end of the tape precisely and stick it down. Hold it in place while you pull 8 to 10 in. of tape from the roll. Lay the tape roll flat against the wall and rotate the roll to tighten and straighten it. Slide your finger across the tape to press down. Use this technique wherever you're masking at a right angle to another surface.

Use extra tape to make perfect inside corners

➤ **Getting two long pieces of tape to meet exactly in the corner is difficult, so don't try.** Don't worry about getting the long pieces of tape to meet in the corner. Start about 3/4 in. from the corner and run them using the previous method. Then go back and finish the corners with small lengths of tape using the technique as shown.

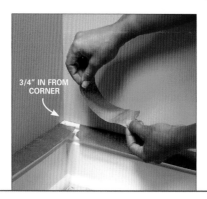

3/4" IN FROM CORNER

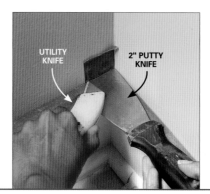

UTILITY KNIFE

2" PUTTY KNIFE

Seal the edge to prevent bleeding paint

➤ **Seal the tape to the surface by pressing it down firmly with the edge of a flexible putty knife as shown.** This is the most important step in good masking and it only takes a few moments. If you skip it, you risk a loose seal that will allow paint to seep underneath. You'll have to scrape off the seeped paint later and touch up the trim.

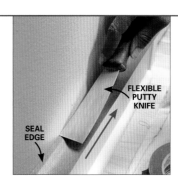

Apply firm pressue but avoid wrinkling or tearing of tape. You don't have to press down the entire width of the tape. Sealing about 1/32 in. along the edge is all that's needed. Hold the putty knife at an angle as shown. This puts pressure along the critical wall edge of the tape.

Use flaps to protect trim from roller spatter

➤ **Extend the painter's tape with a piece of 3-in. masking paper.** It will stand straight out and protect the woodwork from most roller spatter and drips. Apply along the top trim of windows and doors and along the baseboard. Wider paper may seem like a better idea, but it'll sag and won't provide as much protection.

Cut before you remove tape

➤ **Let the paint dry for 24 hours.** Then run a sharp blade along the edge of the tape to slice through the paint film. If you don't do this, the paint film will tear, leaving an ugly, jagged edge. Remove tape at about a 45-degree angle to the painted surface to minimize the tendency for the paint to peel.

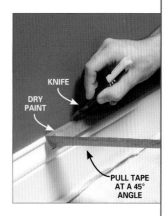

CAUTION: Cheap painter's tape is no bargain. You want tape that will seal tightly to the surface and come off easily. But there's no single type of tape that will work in every circumstance. For general masking, use Scotch-Blue No. 2090. There are two versions: one for standard masking, and one with less adhesion for masking over delicate surfaces. You can leave these on for up to 14 days. You can also use the blue tape on window glass. Scotch No. 2060 is extra-sticky and works well for textured surfaces like stucco and brick. If you're only going to buy one width, get 1-1/2-in.-wide tape. It works well for most tasks.

7

8

7. Smooth the paint along the ceiling using a long horizontal stroke without reloading the roller with paint. If you are skilled enough to roll within an inch of the ceiling while rolling vertically, you can skip this step.

8. Lay paint on wall areas above and below windows and doors with a long horizontal stroke. Then smooth it off with short vertical strokes so the texture will match the rest of the wall.

pro tips!

The best coat of paint can't hide bumpy walls

➤ Fill holes with lightweight spackling compound and sand them smooth when it dries. Then go over the entire wall with 100-grit sandpaper mounted in a drywall sanding handle. The ultimate setup for this job is a pole-mounted drywall sander with a 100-grit mesh drywall sanding screen, but any method of sanding off old paint lumps and bumps will do. Next mask off the baseboard and window and door trim. Slide the blade of a flexible putty knife along the edge of the masking tape to seal it. Otherwise paint will bleed underneath.

pro tips!

Tips for a perfect paint job

➤ **Keep a wet edge.** Keeping a wet edge is crucial to all top-quality paint jobs, whether you're enameling a door, varnishing furniture or rolling paint on a wall. The idea is to plan the sequence of work, and work fast enough so that you're always lapping newly applied paint onto paint that's still wet. If you stop for a break in the middle of a wall, for example, and then start painting after this section has dried, you'll likely see a lap mark where the two areas join. The rolling technique we show avoids this problem by allowing you to quickly cover a large area with paint and then return to smooth it out—which brings us to the second important painting technique.

➤ **Lay it on, smooth it off.** The biggest mistake most beginning painters make, whether they're brushing or rolling, is taking too long to apply the paint. Photo 4 shows how to lay on the paint. Then quickly spread it out and repeat the laying-on process again (Photo 5). This will only work with a good-quality roller cover that holds a lot of paint. Until you're comfortable with the technique and get a feel for how quickly the paint is drying, cover only about 3 or 4 ft. of wall before smoothing the whole area off (Photo 6). If you find the paint is drying slowly, you can cover an entire wall before smoothing it off.

➤ **Get as close as you can.** Since rollers can't get tight to edges, the first painting step is to brush along the ceiling, inside corners and moldings. This "cutting in" process leaves brush marks that won't match the roller texture on the rest of the wall. For the best-looking job, you'll want to cover as many brush marks as possible with the roller. Do this by carefully rolling up close to inside corners, moldings and the ceiling. Face the open end of the roller toward the edge and remember not to use a roller that's fully loaded with paint. With practice, you'll be able to get within an inch of the ceiling rolling vertically, and can avoid crawling up on a ladder to paint horizontally.

➤ **Pick out the lumps before they dry.** It's inevitable that you'll end up with an occasional lump in your paint. Keep the roller cover away from the floor where it might pick up bits of debris that are later spread against the wall. Drying bits of paint from the edge of the bucket or bucket screen can also cause this problem. Cover the bucket with a damp cloth when you're not using it. If partially dried paint is sloughing off the screen, take it out and clean it. Keep a wet rag in your pocket and pick lumps off the wall as you go. Strain used paint through a mesh paint strainer to remove lumps. Five-gallon size strainers are available at paint stores for about $1.

➤ **Scrape excess paint from the roller before you wash it.** Use your putty knife, or better yet, a special roller-scraping tool with a semicircular cutout in the blade. Then rinse the roller cover until the water runs clear. A roller and paint brush spinning tool, available at hardware and paint stores for about $8, simplifies the cleaning task. Just slip the roller cover onto the spinner and repeatedly wet and spin out the roller until it's clean.

How to caulk a tub

When the caulking around a bathtub starts to crack and become a cozy home for dark stains that signal mold, it's time to replace it. The caulk is the watertight seal between the bathtub and the wall. Once the caulk's integrity is compromised, water can invade the wall, causing rot in the framing around the tub. Save yourself an expensive repair—you can replace old caulk in less than an hour at almost no cost.

1. Loosen the old caulk. Push a razor scraper in all the way under both edges of the old caulk bead to release its grip. Don't pry the caulk with the scraper because you could break off the razor blade.

2. Scrape the loosened caulk out of the joint with the pointed end of a can opener or putty knife. Once the old grout is removed and you have a clean, dry surface you can apply the new caulk.

3. Tubs sink a bit when full, so fill before you caulk, and leave until the bead has cured. This will keep a seal joint from cracking when weight is applied.

4. Using a utility knife, cut the nozzle tip of the caulk tube at a 45-degree angle so the opening is about the diameter of a wire coat hanger. Smooth and round the cut tip with sandpaper.

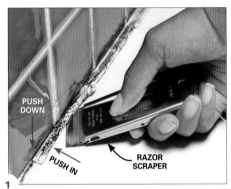

5

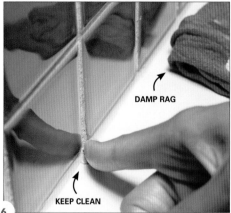

DAMP RAG

KEEP CLEAN

6

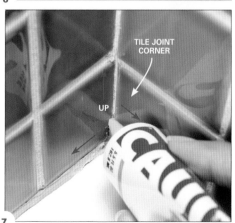

TILE JOINT CORNER

UP

7

5. Pull the caulk tube down the tub joint from the inside corner of the tub. Keep even pressure on the tube by pushing the caulk forward and folding over the empty portion. The bead should be sized so only a slight amount wipes off when you drag your finger over it.

6. Dampen your finger and drag it over the freshly laid bead of caulk. Press the caulk into the joint with the tip of your finger and scrape away the excess with the sides of your finger (it may take a few swipes). Wipe excess caulk off your finger with a damp rag. Note: For acrylic/latex caulk, dip your finger in water. With silicone, slip on a surgical-style glove and use alcohol.

7. Include the tile corner joint. Caulk up the tile corner joint if the old caulk has cracked or deteriorated.

8. Allow the caulk to dry. Then empty the tub but wait 24 hours before using.

pro tips!

➤ Tubs and showers require a caulk that contains mold and mildew prevention additives—labeled "for kitchen and bath use." Most are 100 percent silicone, but you can also find some latex versions.

➤ Test the caulk. Most caulks and sealants have a shelf life of one to two years, but few companies bother to supply a freshness date. So take the time to test the product on a non-porous surface, such as a spare tile or a clean piece of glass, to be sure it will flow smoothly, adhere and cure. If the caulk is not fresh, you could recaulk your entire bathroom only to find that the caulk, which should begin curing in a few hours, is still not cured after three days.

➤ Replace silicone with silicone. Nothing else will stick to silicone, or where silicone has been, but more silicone. To find out if the old caulk is silicone, clean off a section of the old caulk, let it dry, and try sticking Scotch tape to it. If the tape doesn't stick, the caulk is probably silicone.

PROFESSIONAL COST: $200

YOUR COST: $30

SAVINGS: $170

COMPLEXITY
Simple

TOOLS
Straightedge
Utility knife
Paint scraper or
  putty knife
Small notched
  applicator
Rolling pin

MATERIALS
Patch of flooring
Vinyl flooring
  adhesive
Seam-sealing kit

Patch a vinyl floor

You can usually fix a small slice or tear in your sheet vinyl floor by lifting the loose edges, applying a little vinyl flooring adhesive and then placing a weight over the repair. But for burns or major injuries, a transplant is the solution. Get everything you need at a home center or a flooring store for less than $30.

1. Using a straightedge and sharp utility knife, carefully cut out the damaged area. If your flooring design has faux grout lines in it, as most do, cut along the edges of the lines.

2. Peel up the damaged section and remove the old backing and adhesive with a paint scraper or putty knife. A hair dryer or heat gun (set on "low") will soften the adhesive.

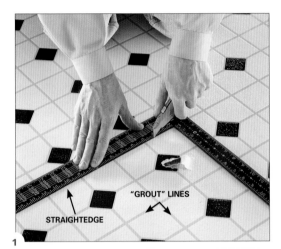

"GROUT" LINES

STRAIGHTEDGE

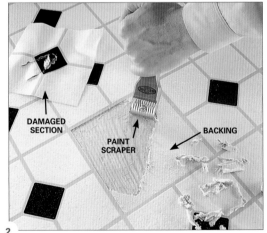

DAMAGED
SECTION

PAINT
SCRAPER

BACKING

CAUTION:
Some sheet vinyl floors are glued down only around the perimeter and can't be repaired using the method shown. To determine how your vinyl is glued down, cut a 1/2-in. slit in a hidden spot (at least 8 in. from the floor's perimeter) and probe the underside with a screwdriver. You'll be able to feel if it's attached.

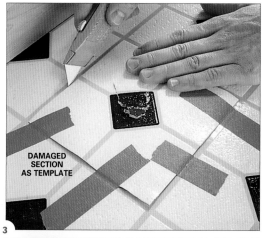

DAMAGED SECTION AS TEMPLATE

3

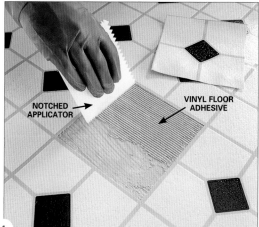

NOTCHED APPLICATOR

VINYL FLOOR ADHESIVE

4

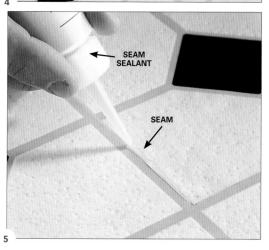

SEAM SEALANT

SEAM

5

3. Matching the pattern precisely, tape the cut-out damaged piece over the scrap, and use the damaged piece as a template for cutting the new patch to size. Test the fit of the patch.

4. Spread adhesive on the floor with a small notched applicator.

5. Set the patch in place and use a rolling pin to force out any air pockets under the patch. Give the adhesive time to set, then apply a vinyl seam sealant to the seams. Different adhesives and seam sealants require slightly different treatment; be sure to follow the manufacturer's directions for both.

pro tips!

➤ If you don't have a leftover scrap of flooring gathering dust in the basement, you'll have to cut the patch material out of your floor—from the back of a closet or under the fridge, for example.

COMPLEXITY
Moderate

TOOLS
Cold chisel
Hammer
Grout saw
Notched trowel
Rubber groat float
Screwdriver

MATERIALS
Replacement tile
Safety glasses
Gloves
Thin-set mortar
Short length of wood
Grout sponge

Replace a damaged floor tile

When a tile chips or breaks, the only way to fix it is to replace it. The total repair time will be around two hours, spread over a couple of days. Most of your time will be spent on the first day removing the damaged tile, the grout and the old adhesive and then installing the new tile. The final step (done a day or two later) is regrouting around the new tile.

1. Remove the damaged tile with a cold chisel and hammer. Start at the edge of the tile, in the grout. Ceramic tile is brittle—small pieces will fly! Wear safety glasses and gloves. Be careful not to chip the surrounding tiles.

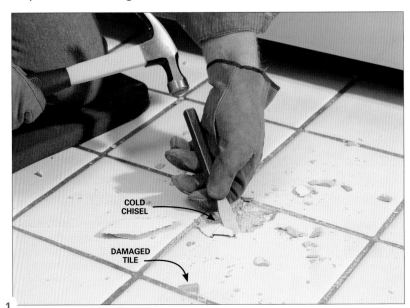

COLD
CHISEL

DAMAGED
TILE

1

pro tips!

Matching the tile and grout

➤ If you're lucky, you'll have some extra tiles. If you don't have extras, visit some tile stores. You might be able to find a close match. If you can't find anything close, you can get creative and replace a few more tiles to make a new pattern.

➤ Matching the grout can be a bit tricky, even though tile stores carry a wide range of colors. For the best match, take a piece of the old grout with you to the tile store.

➤ Mix some grout before you start the project to make sure the color matches. Grout changes color as it dries and you may find you'll need to do some color adjusting by mixing two colors.

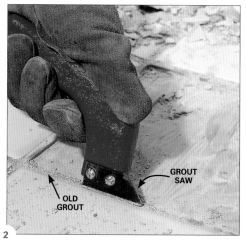

OLD GROUT

GROUT SAW

2

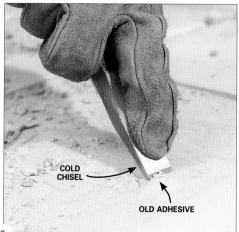

COLD CHISEL

OLD ADHESIVE

3

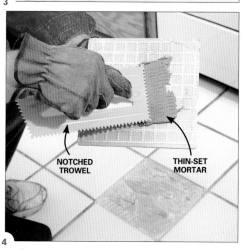

NOTCHED TROWEL

THIN-SET MORTAR

4

2. Remove the old grout with a grout saw. Some of the grout can be chipped out with the chisel; however, you'll need to saw away all of the old grout to ensure a proper fit for the new tile.

3. Scrape off the old adhesive with a cold chisel. Get rid of as much as possible so the new tile will adhere properly and lie flat. Scraping is the best way to remove old adhesive. Don't use a heat gun or solvent unless you want a big mess.

4. Apply the adhesive (thin-set mortar) with a notched trowel on the back of the tile. Be sure to spread the adhesive out to the edges. Don't skimp on the adhesive: Too little will make the tile sit lower than the surrounding tiles. Any excess adhesive wil! ooze out and can be removed after the next step.

CAUTION:
Always check the adhesive package for the required drying time before applying the new grout. If you rush the regrouting step and the tile shifts, you'll need to start over.

NEW TILE

SCRAP WOOD

5

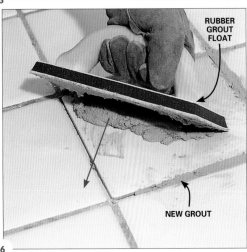

RUBBER GROUT FLOAT

NEW GROUT

6

5. Place the tile, making sure that the grout lines are even with the adjacent tiles. To set the tile firmly into the adhesive, use a short length of wood and gently tap it with a hammer. If the tile is lower than the surrounding tiles, simply remove it, apply additional adhesive and then reset the tile. Scrape out any excess adhesive from between the tiles with a screwdriver. Once the tile is set, stay off it until the adhesive is dry, usually 24 hours.

6. Spread the grout using a rubber grout float. Hold the float at a 45-degree angle to the tile. Move the grout in both directions at an angle to the grout lines to make sure it fills the gaps between the tiles. Let the grout set for about 10 minutes and then wipe the area with a damp grout sponge. A grout sponge has rounded corners and is the best way to shape the grout lines. Once the grout has dried, usually overnight, wipe off any residue with a soft cloth.

Repair carpet snags

If you have a running snag in carpet with woven loops, don't worry. You can make a repair so perfect that it will be invisible to everyone but you. All it takes is scissors, a small screwdriver, tape and some carpet adhesive, which is available at home centers.

....

1. Gently tug the loose yarn to find the point where it's still firmly attached to the backing. Snip it off as close to the backing as possible and save it.

2. Protect nearby carpet by masking off repair area with painters tape. Squeeze a heavy bead of carpet seam sealer into the run. Use a screwdriver to press each "scab"of the saved yarn's dried glue into the carpet's backing and seam sealer until a loop is reestablished.

1

SEAM
SEALER

2

PROFESSIONAL
COST: $75

YOUR COST: $6

SAVINGS: $69

COMPLEXITY
Simple

TOOLS
Scissors
Small screwdriver

MATERIALS
Painters tape
Carpet seam sealer

DIY carpet cleaning

Carpet pros do a more thorough job than you can, but hiring a pro is expensive. So the next-best approach is to alternate between DIY and pro cleanings. DIY "steam"-cleaning machines can be effective if you understand how to use them and take the time to clean your carpet carefully.

Most rental machines weigh more, hold more water and come with a wider wand than purchased models, making them useful for larger, high-traffic areas. Purchased models are usually smaller, more portable and easier to store. They're good for spot cleaning and are easier to drag up and down stairs.

1. Vacuum beforehand to remove large particles of soil. Then use the DIY machine as per manufacturer's instructions. Be careful and take your time. Hurrying through a cleaning will leave soap residue, a soaked carpet and a pad that can mold or mildew. Larger rental machines require you to pull them across the floor rather than push.

CAUTION:
➤ Don't overwet the carpet. DIY machines put a lot of moisture into the carpet, and most don't have strong enough suction to extract it thoroughly. Make only one pass with the soap and water solution. Make one pass with the neutralizing rinse solution. Then make two or three drying passes with the water off.

pro tips!

➤ You can rent a steam cleaner from a grocery store or home center. If you pick the machine up late in the day, many stores will charge you a half-day rate and let you keep the machine until the next morning. Don't forget to buy the detergent!

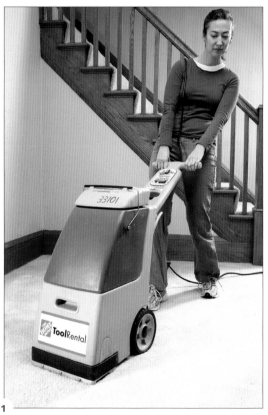

1

2

3

2. Use less soap than directed.The soap used in DIY machines foams a lot and leaves behind a lot of residue, which acts as a dirt magnet. Despite what the directions say, use a tablespoon or less of soap to 1 gallon of hot water to prevent soap residue. Make one pass.

3. Use a mild acid rinse to neutralize soap residue. DIY machines are often sold with a neutralizing rinse, or you can make your own using 1 cup white vinegar to 1 gallon hot water. Rinse after you make one pass with the detergent solution. Let dry completely.

4. Vacuum again after you clean and the carpet is completely dry to pick up soil that wicks to the surface during drying.

pro tips!

➤ Clean the carpet before it becomes really dirty. How often your carpet needs cleaning depends on the kind of carpet traffic you have (think kids and pets). Clean the carpet when the color starts looking dull. If you wait until the carpet is filthy, cleaning it will be much more difficult, take much longer and cost more.

➤ Pretreat stains and high-traffic areas. Mix a drop of detergent with hot water in a spray bottle and lightly mist the dirtiest areas. Let sit 5 to 10 minutes before starting the general cleaning.

➤ Remove or elevate furniture. If your furniture is too heavy to move, put aluminum foil squares, wood blocks or plastic film under and around the legs of all furniture to prevent rust from metal casters or stains from paint and finishes from transferring to damp carpet.

➤ Let it dry thoroughly. Wet carpet is a perfect environment for mold and mildew. After you clean your carpets, open the windows, use fans and a dehumidifier, or put the AC on a moderate setting (72 to 78 degrees) to remove excess moisture from the air. Don't replace the furniture or walk on the carpet until it's completely dry. This can take up to 12 hours, though six to eight hours is typical.

Cleaning

PROFESSIONAL
COST: $25

YOUR COST: $15

SAVINGS: $10

COMPLEXITY
Simple

TOOLS
Rags
Rubber gloves

MATERIALS
Baking soda
Nail polish remover
Countertop polish

CAUTION:
Check the label
and make sure any
product you use
is recommended
for laminate
countertops.

Remove stains from plastic laminate countertops

Get tough on plastic laminate stains. Using the right cleaner and having some patience will make even the most stubborn stains go away. Just follow our advice and you'll get rid of those ugly stains for good.

1. Apply a baking soda paste to the stain. Mix baking soda with just enough water to form a thick paste. Apply the paste to the stain and lay a wet paper towel over the paste to keep it moist. Baking soda is slightly abrasive and can leave fine scratches, so don't scrub. Just let the paste work for one to two hours and then wipe it off gently. Baking soda paste often removes stains left by fruit juices and other liquids.

CAUTION:
Don't clean laminate with abrasives like steel wool, scouring pads or scouring powder. They may remove stains, but they may also leave micro-scratches in the surface, making future stains more likely.

pro tips!

➤ Don't let any type of cleaner or solvent pool over seams in the laminate or along the edges. It can seep under the laminate, weaken the adhesive and damage the particleboard substrate.

NAIL POLISH REMOVER

2

COUNTERTOP POLISH

3

2. For tough stains use nail polish remover. Nail polish remover won't harm or discolor plastic laminate, but play it safe and test on an inconspicuous spot first. Wet a rag or cotton ball with nail polish remover and rub. Use white rags to avoid staining the countertop with fabric dye. **Caution:** This solvent is flammable.

3. The best way to prevent stains is to wipe up messes immediately; the longer something sits, the more likely it is to leave a stain. A coating of countertop polish can also help. (Coating products usually aren't necessary on newer laminate.)

   Spray or wipe on a product meant for countertops and wipe off the excess. Years of wear leave surfaces more porous and stain-prone; that's when these protective coatings can make a big difference. Any coating product will wear off and should be reapplied every few weeks.

CAUTION: Bleach?

There's no doubt that bleach is a great stain remover. Some laminate manufacturers suggest using it undiluted on stains, while others warn against using any product that contains bleach.

Since you may not know what brand of laminate you have, test bleach before using it. Wipe a little on an inconspicuous spot and let it dry. Check the spot for discoloration before you use bleach on a stain.

PROFESSIONAL
COST: $25

YOUR COST: $0

SAVINGS: $25

COMPLEXITY
Simple

MATERIALS
Toothbrush

Anti-bacterial grease-
  cutting kitchen
  cleanse

Orange or lemon
  peels

Clean a stinky garbage disposer

Does your kitchen sink smell bad? Is it coming from your garbage disposer? Here's how to clean a garbage disposer and get rid of those disgusting odors.

Even if you run your garbage disposer until the last shred of food is gone, and you let the water run the recommended time, you can still wind up with an out-of-control science experiment that stinks up your kitchen. Here's the key: Clean under the splash guard and the chamber.

1. Cleaning the splash guard is easier than you think. You don't even have to remove it. Dip an old toothbrush in antibacterial grease-cutting kitchen cleaner (Clorox Antibacterial Degreaser is one choice) and lift up one corner of the splash guard. Scrub off the crud and rinse with cold water. Repeat with each flap until it's totally clean and rinsed. Then submit your resignation to the stink patrol.

Sometimes the splash guard is ripped, broken or just too dirty to clean and needs to be replaced. Don't worry, it's not that big a deal. See **How to replace a garbage disposer splash guard** (page 88) to learn how easy that job is.

1

2

2. To clean the chamber, run water at about half-throttle and drop in orange or lemon peels. Run the disposer for five seconds. Citric acid from the peels softens crusty waste and attacks smelly bacteria. Give the acid about 15 minutes to do its work.

3. Turn on the water and the disposer and drop in a few ice cubes. Place stopper on top. Flying shards of ice work like a sandblaster inside the disposer.

4. Run the water until the bowl is about half-full. Then pull the stopper and turn on the disposer to flush it out.

How to clean oven door glass

It's a mystery how baking slop gets deposited between oven door glass panels. Cleaning them out looks impossible, but all you really need to do is dissassemble the door. It's simple and takes less than an hour. Really.

PROFESSIONAL
COST: $110

YOUR COST: $5

SAVINGS: $105

COMPLEXITY
Simple

TOOLS
4-in-1 screwdriver

MATERIALS
Rubber gloves
Nylon scrub pad
Degreaser
Glass cleaner
Paper towels

1. Remove the oven door (consult the manual for how to unlock the hinges and lift the door off). Then remove the exterior trim panel by removing the screws that secure the front panel to the oven door frame. Note their location and store them in a cup. Then carefully lift off the panel and set it aside.

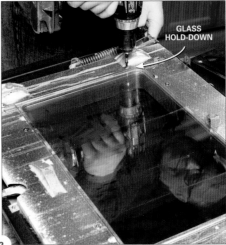

2. Remove the glass. Remove the screws from the glass hold-downs and set them aside. Note the location of the retaining tabs above and below the glass. Lift out the glass and handle it carefully (it's expensive and breaks easily!) and clean it.

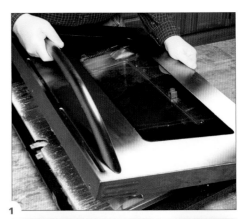

GLASS HOLD-DOWN

3. Clean off the crud with a nylon scrub pad, hot water and degreaser. Rinse and dry, then clean with glass cleaner. Wear gloves to prevent fingerprints as you place the glass back onto the oven door. Be sure the glass sits inside the locating tabs before you reassemble the hold-downs. Then install the hold-down channels and screws and the trim panel. Put the door back on the oven.

Clean range hood grease filters with a degreaser

Running your vent hood grease filter through the dishwasher can yield disappointing results. Likewise with "grease cutting" household cleaners. Clean the stubborn grease from your range hood filter quickly and easily with a mixture of auto water-based degreaser and water.

1. Fill the sink with hot water and degreaser, drop in the filter and let the degreaser do all the work. The filter will come out sparkling clean in just a few minutes.

2. Rinse it off and let dry.

1

PROFESSIONAL COST: $15

YOUR COST: $6

SAVINGS: $9

COMPLEXITY
Simple

MATERIALS
Rubber gloves
Auto water-based degreaser

PROFESSIONAL
COST: $15

YOUR COST: $4

SAVINGS: $11

COMPLEXITY
Simple

MATERIALS
Sponge or cloth
Rubber gloves
All-purpose cleaner
  containing orange
  oil

Clean kitchen cabinets

Grease and dirt build up on kitchen cabinets over time. No need to have them refinished—give them a great cleaning!

1. Heat a slightly damp sponge or cloth in the microwave for 20 to 30 seconds until it's hot. Careful not to burn yourself when removing.

2. Put on a pair of rubber gloves, spray the cabinets with an all-purpose cleaner containing orange oil. For stubborn spots, let the cleaner sit for five minutes first.

1

3

3. Wipe off the cleaner with the hot sponge. Wipe in the direction of the wood grain. Rinse and reheat the sponge as it becomes saturated. Then wipe the cabinets with a cool, damp cloth. The orange oil leaves a shiny coating. This works for any wood or metal surface.

Microwave—steam away messes

Your microwave still cooks but the baked-on food and spills have you thinking it's time to replace it. Wait—it's easier to clean than you think.

PROFESSIONAL
COST: $15

YOUR COST: $0

SAVINGS: $15

COMPLEXITY
Simple

MATERIALS
Measuring cup
Lemon
Sponge

1. Partially fill a measuring or coffee cup with water and add a slice of lemon. Boil the water for a minute, and then leave the door closed and let the steam loosen the mess.

2. After 10 minutes, open the door and remove the cup. Take out the turntable to clean it, then wipe down the top, bottom, sides, and door of the microwave before putting it back.

1

pro tips!

➤ Sterilize sponges. Your dish sponge smells like last night's dinner, and detergent won't help. Time to toss it, right? Wrong. Pour a dash of white vinegar or lemon juice in a bowl of water, soak the sponge and then heat it in the microwave on high for a minute. The heat will deodorize and disinfect the sponge—even after wiping up raw egg or chicken.

PROFESSIONAL
COST: $120

YOUR COST: $10

SAVINGS: $110

COMPLEXITY
Simple

TOOLS
Wet/dry vaccum

MATERIALS
Carpet stain
  removal product or
  homemade solution
White cloth
Small silicone brush
  or spray bottle

CAUTION:
After sucking up as
much of the spill
as possible, resist
the temptation to
hit the stain with
strong cleaners
like vinegar and
hydrogen peroxide
right out of the
gate. Those
products can set
the stain and even
discolor your
carpet.

How to get red wine, coffee, and tomato sauce stains out of carpets

Getting as much of the liquid and solids out of the carpet as quickly as possible is the single most important part of removing a carpet stain. But blotting and scooping can actually drive the stain deep into the carpet backing and pad. Instead, reach for your wet/dry vacuum and vacuum up the spill. Convert your wet/dry vac to wet mode by removing the paper filter and installing a foam cover (if equipped) before sucking anything up.

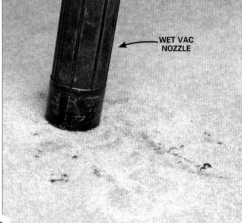

WET VAC
NOZZLE

1. Suck up the mess. Push the hose directly onto the carpet fibers and leave it in place for several seconds. Don't rub or drag the hose over the carpet. Move to an adjoining spot and repeat as many times as required to remove as much of the spill as possible.

1

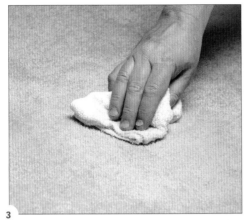

3

4

5

2. Apply a cleaning solution. Use a store-bought carpet stain removal product or make your own by mixing 1/4 teaspoon dish soap (clear is best) to 1 cup of water. Pour the homemade solution into a spray bottle and apply a generous amount to the soiled area, but don't saturate it. Let the cleaning solution soak into the fibers for a few minutes before moving on to the next step.

3. Blot gently. Fold a clean white cloth (dyed fabric can transfer color to the carpet) into a small square and dab the carpet, starting at the outside edge. Roll the cloth toward the center and refold the cloth to a clean section as you soak up more stain.

   Your goal is to move the carpet fibers, spread the cleaner slightly, and soak up the stain. Avoid aggressive blotting. That just drives the stain deeper into the pile, backing and padding. After blotting, use your wet/dry vac again to remove as much cleaning solution as possible.

4. Rinse the stained area. Dab or spray clean water onto the stained area. Never pour water directly onto the carpet—it'll push the cleaning solution into the backing and padding and can cause mold.

   Don't leave cleaning solution in the carpet. Leftover chemicals attract dirt, causing the spot to get soiled faster than the rest of the carpet. So rinse the stained area multiple times with clear water.

   Vacuum the rinse water between applications until you remove as much final rinse water as possible.

5. Clean your shop vacuum right away. Dump some disinfecting cleaner into a bucket of warm water and drop your hose into it. Empty the tank and rinse both the hose and tank with water.

CAUTION:
Pet vomit and fecal and urine stains require additional neutralization and disinfection steps.

PROFESSIONAL
COST: $20

YOUR COST: $0

SAVINGS: $20

COMPLEXITY
Simple

TOOLS
Iron

MATERIALS
Butter knife
Heavy-duty carpet
  cleaner
Spoon
White cotton towels

CAUTION:
Do not iron over a
paper bag. It can
overheat and burn
the carpet, and
should not be used
to remove wax.

How to remove wax from a carpet

Candle wax accidentally dripped on a plush carpet may look like a hopeless mess, but with a cool head, a hot iron and a few tricks of the trade, you can make a big wax mess disappear.

1. Scrape the hardened wax loose with a butter knife (be gentle with Berber carpets; the loops fray easily). Vacuum up the loose wax and scrape off any remaining wax chunks.

   Scraping the knife against the carpet will probably leave the area a little fuzzy. To remove the fuzz, lay a scissors flat on the carpet. Push down lightly on the pivot of the scissors and trim off any fuzz.

2

3

2. Dampen a white cotton towel, fold it in half and place it over the wax. Press an iron set on "high" over the towel for 10 seconds. The heat will draw the wax out of the carpet and into the towel. Repeat until the wax is gone (you may have to hold the iron in place for up to 30 seconds). If the towel dries out, rewet it, and if it becomes loaded with wax, grab another one.

3. There's a good chance the wax will discolor the area, especially in a light-colored carpet. Take out the spot with heavy-duty carpet stain remover. Spray carpet cleaner on the stain and rub it into the carpet with a spoon. Dab it dry with a clean white towel, then let the carpet air-dry (it will appear slightly darker until completely dry). Light-colored carpets and dark stains may require several scrubbings.

Carpet cleaning tips for pet owners

Many pet owners do exactly what they shouldn't do when they clean up pet messes. But if you learn how to clean up the right way, with the right products, you can prevent a permanent stain. You'll get the best results if you have the products and a carpet extractor in hand when you discover the accident.

1. Buy a handheld extractor to suck liquids from the carpet. Hit the carpet as soon as possible and vacuum like there's no tomorrow.
   Warning: Using paper towels or rags to blot up urine and vomit soaks up the surface liquid but still leaves a lot in the carpet. And stomping on those paper towels only makes it worse. That forces the liquid deeper into the padding and then into the subflooring. Instead, invest in a handheld carpet extractor. Don't use a shop vacuum—the smell will linger in the filter and it's much harder to clean than a small extractor.

CARPET
EXTRACTOR

1

2. To finish cleaning up a urine stain, fresh or dried, use a urine-specific bio-enzymatic cleaner. It neutralizes the urea and uric acid and eliminates proteins and starches. Ordinary carpet cleaners can't do that. In fact, using a carpet cleaner before a bio-enzymatic cleaner can set the stain permanently. Liquid messes spread as they're absorbed into the carpet, so always treat a larger area than the original stain.

3. For solids, sink the edge of the putty knife into the carpet at the edge of the mess. Then push it forward to scrape the solid waste up and into the dustpan. Scooping up the solids with paper towels or rags can actually force them into the carpet.

3

4. For all solid messes, saturate the stain with an oxygenated bio-enzymatic cleaner. Let it sit for 45 minutes to separate additional solids from the carpet fibers. Then clean up those solids. Bio-enzymatic cleaners take a long time to work. Just let the treated area air-dry. Then use the handheld extractor vacuum to raise the nap.

pro tips!

More about cleaning solutions

➤ Home remedies that use vinegar and baking soda simply mask the odor for a short time and don't eliminate the cause. Instead, buy a product made for your particular type of pet mess.

➤ Commercial pet cleaning products range from a few dollars to more than $20 per quart. The least expensive products usually contain a carpet detergent for the stain and an odor-masking chemical. Since they don't actually neutralize the substance, the smell usually returns on humid days.

➤ Spend more to get a product with enzymes. These products are good for small surface stains. But if you're dealing with a large stain, one that has soaked deep into the carpet or one that has already dried, spend more yet and use a product with bacteria, enzymes and an oxygen booster.

Clean wood with mineral spirits

Polish buildup and dirt embedded in wood can muddy the finish. Take a tip from furniture restorers and clean it with mineral spirits. Mineral spirits is a gentle solvent that dissolves years of grime and residue from cleaners or polishes without harming wood finishes. Get it at a home center or paint store.

1. Soak a soft, absorbent, clean cloth with mineral spirits and wipe the finish. Work in a well-ventilated area and remember that the fumes are flammable. Keep applying and wiping until the cloth no longer picks up dirt. Then do a final wipe with a fresh, clean rag.

    Hang the cloth outdoors to dry before throwing it in the trash.

2. Clean crevices, grooves and carved areas with cotton swabs dipped in mineral spirits.

Erase white rings

Spilled water or a wet glass can leave a white stain on wood furniture. Often, complete stripping and refinishing are the only solution. But sometimes you can remove water marks in a few minutes without harming the finish quickly with petroleum jelly or one of these solvents. Both solvents give off nasty fumes, so work outside in a well-ventilated area. If you think the piece might be especially old or valuable, consult an antiques dealer before trying these remedies.

1. Slather petroleum jelly on the ring and let it sit overnight. Often, the oil in the jelly will penetrate the finish and render the ring invisible. If that doesn't work, go on to try one of the solvents.

PETROLEUM JELLY

1

2. Rub the stain with a soft rag dipped in mineral spirits. If the original finish has a coating of wax over it, there's a good chance that only the wax has turned white. Mineral spirits removes wax without harming the underlying finish. Have patience; the mineral spirits may take a few minutes to soften the wax. If the stain disappears but leaves the rubbed area looking dull, clean the entire surface with mineral spirits and apply a new coat of furniture wax.

3. If mineral spirits doesn't work, gently wipe the stain using a soft rag lightly dampened with denatured alcohol. Alcohol can damage some finishes, so test it on an inconspicuous spot first. Stop every minute or so to examine the finish to make sure you're not damaging it. Again, have patience. Sometimes alcohol can draw out moisture that's trapped in the finish, but it works slowly. If you don't see any results after five minutes, refinishing is the only way to remove the mark.

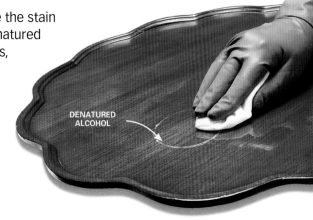

DENATURED ALCOHOL

COMPLEXITY
Simple

MATERIALS
Rubber gloves
Rags
Mineral spirits
Fine-tip brown
  marker
Paste wax

Polish and renew wood furniture

If you have wood furniture that's looking dull, don't rush to a refinisher; revive the shine with paste wax. Wax is a more durable coating than liquid furniture polish and it won't attract dust as many polishes do. Wax will fill and hide very fine scratches, but it won't hide dents or deeper scratches.

1. Clean the wood using a soft cloth dampened with mineral spirits to remove grime as well as residue left by furniture polishes. Open windows for ventilation. When the mineral spirits dries, buff off any residue with a dry cloth. Touch up scratches with a fine-tip marker before you wax. Visit an art supply store to find a wide array of browns.

2. Wrap a walnut-sized ball of wax in a cloth. As you rub with the ball, wax will ooze through the rag. Rub on the wax in a circular pattern. Apply only enough wax to form a thin gloss—a heavy coat just leaves you with more wax to buff off later. If you haven't used wax before and you're working on a large piece of furniture, wax and then buff small areas no more than 3 x 3 ft.

WAX BALL

3. Don't wait for the wax to dry completely and form a haze the way you would with car wax. Fully dried furniture wax is very hard to buff smooth. Wait only until the wax partially dries and begins to look dull (typically 15 to 30 minutes). Then rub the surface with a cotton cloth to remove the excess wax. The rag should glide smoothly over the wax with only a little elbow grease. Turn and refold the cloth frequently to expose clean cloth.

   If you've waited too long and can't rub out the swirls of wax, simply apply more wax, then wait and wipe again (solvent in the second coat of wax will soften the first coat).

3

4. A wax finish doesn't require any special care; simply dust with a dry or damp cloth. A wax coating will last months or even years depending on how heavily the furniture is used. When the finish again looks worn, scuffed or dirty, just clean and rewax. Don't worry about wax buildup. Each new wax job dissolves and removes much of the previous coat.

pro tips!

➤ Wax is available in several colors. Most home centers and hardware stores carry only light-colored wax, which is fine for most finishes. But don't use light wax on dark finishes that have recesses in the grain.

Yellowish wax that fills the tiny crevices in the surface will look bad. (This won't happen on glossy, solid dark finishes.) For wax in a variety of colors, check woodworking and paint stores and online suppliers. You can also use dark wax to deepen the color of a finish.

PROFESSIONAL
COST: $150

YOUR COST: $20

SAVINGS: $130

COMPLEXITY
Simple

MATERIALS
Rubber gloves
Bleach
Scrubber brush
Stain-blocking primer
Paintbrush
Paint with
  mildewcide

CAUTION:
A few types of
mold are highly
toxic. If you have
an allergic reaction
to mold or a heavy
infestation inside
your home, call in
a pro to analyze
the types.

Attack closet mildew

Closets are often cool, damp and dark—fungus paradise. Here's how to deal
with mold and mildew in closets or on other walls.

1. Determine if it's mold or dirt on the walls. Most mold is
   unmistakable, but sometimes it just makes a surface look dirty.
   For a quick test, dip a swab in diluted bleach (1 part bleach,
   16 parts water) and dab it on the wall. If the spot quickly lightens
   (or keeps coming back after cleaning), assume it's mold.
       Mold test kits are available that detect the presence and
   identify the type of mold, but they won't help determine the
   cause or what to do about it.

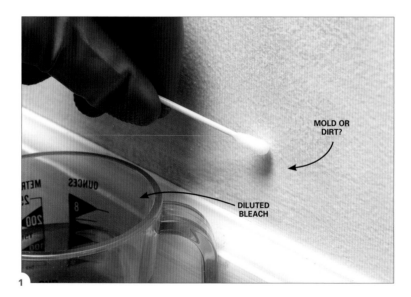

MOLD OR DIRT?

DILUTED BLEACH

CAUTION:
Don't mix ammonia or any detergent containing ammonia
with bleach. The combination forms a poisonous gas.

2

2. To clean and kill mildew, mix three parts of water and one part bleach. Scrub thoroughly, but don't worry if the stains don't completely disappear.

3. Prime the area. Mildew stains can bleed through paint, so coat the area with a stain-blocking primer before painting.

4. Add mildewcide to paint or use paint that already contains mildewcide (check the label).

pro tips!

➤ Run a dehumidifier in damp rooms.

➤ Cut closet humidity. Chemical dehumidifiers are nontoxic products that absorb moisture from the air.

➤ Leave closet doors open or replace solid doors with louvered doors to increase airflow.

3

CHEMICAL DEHUMIDIFIER

PAINT WITH MILDEWCIDE

MILDEWCIDE ADDITIVE

4

Remove soap scum from tile

PROFESSIONAL COST: $110

YOUR COST: $15

SAVINGS: $95

COMPLEXITY
Simple

MATERIALS
Bucket

Non-scratch nylon scrubber

Nylon grout brush

Glass cleaner

Bleach-containing, nonabrasive soap scum cleaner

Squeegee

Numerous cleaners are available to remove soap scum from tile. But if you face layers of soap scum buildup, stick with an effective bleach-containing, nonabrasive product.

Scum cleaners commonly contain bleach (sodium hypochlorite), which effectively cuts through soap scum and kills mildew. Be sure to READ THE PRODUCT LABEL and match it to the material (tile, fiberglass, etc.) being cleaned.

1. Coat the entire tiled surface (grout, caulk and all) with an all-purpose cleaner that attacks soap scum. Wait 5 to 10 minutes to allow the product to work, which saves your scrubbing elbow.

2. Remove remaining visible scum and deposits by applying light pressure with a non-scratch nylon scrubber. Reapply product to difficult areas and scrub until clean.

3. Remove stains and deposits on grout or caulk by lightly scrubbing back and forth with a grout brush or old toothbrush. Reapply product as needed.

4. Rinse the entire tiled surface thoroughly with a dripping-wet sponge. Push it back and forth across the top of the wall so rinse water streams to the bottom of the wall. Repeat until all cleaner is removed. Then, start at the top of the tile with a bathroom squeegee and move downward to remove as much water as possible.

pro tips!

Microfiber cloths

➤ **Throw out the old cotton rags and the paper towels you use to clean with and use microfiber cloths instead.** These cloths are composed of ultrafine synthetic fibers that are woven together to create a "microfiber." The fibers rub together during cleaning, creating a static charge that attracts dirt and dust, so you can tackle dusting chores without using sprays or chemicals (although you can still use them if you want). The tiny fibers have sharp edges that scour well, but they aren't abrasive, so they won't scratch surfaces. Use the cloths for cleaning appliances, sinks, showers, and TV and computer monitors, and for drying dishes, washing windows and any other chore that requires a cloth (wet or dry). Microfiber cloths leave a streak- and lint-free finish, are very absorbent, and can be washed and reused.

You'll find microfiber cloths wherever cleaning supplies are sold. You can also buy them in bulk at wholesale clubs and use them throughout your house for all kinds of other cleaning chores.

➤ **Polish with a microfiber cloth.** For that finishing touch—after cleaning surfaces with your favorite cleaning solution and drying them off with a microfiber cloth, polish them to a mirror finish with a dry microfiber cloth. Microfiber cloths are perfect for this because they pick up dust, wipe off smudges and don't shed any fibers.

Protect your shower doors from mineral buildup

When the beads of water left on your glass shower door dry out, they leave minerals behind that are at best unsightly, and at worst can be tough as nails to remove if you let them build up. You can avoid beading water altogether by coating the glass with an auto-glass treatment

PROFESSIONAL
COST: $75

YOUR COST: $20

SAVINGS: $55

COMPLEXITY
Simple

TOOLS
Squeegee

MATERIALS
Glass cleaner
Magic Eraser
Auto-glass treatment
 & rain repellent
Microfiber cloth

1. Start by cleaning any mold, mildew or streaks off the glass with a glass cleaner. Use a Mr. Clean Magic Eraser to get into the cracks in textured glass. Scrape off tough buildup with a razor blade.

2. Dry the doors with a microfiber cloth.

3. Treat the doors with a water-repellent product like Aquapel or Rain-X (available at auto parts stores and home centers). Follow the instructions on the package to apply the treatment to your shower door glass. These glass treatments form an invisible film on the glass to increase water repellency, causing water and soap to bead up and run off the glass. (Squeegee off the water after bathing to keep soap scum from building up again.) Spray or wipe on the glass treatment, then wipe it off with a microfiber cloth. Overspray won't harm surrounding surfaces. The products repel water for six months.

3

How to whiten grimy grout

PROFESSIONAL COST: $100

YOUR COST: $10

SAVINGS: $90

COMPLEXITY
Simple

MATERIALS
Sponge
Chamois (2 to 3)
Rubber gloves
DAP Kwik Seal Grout
  Recolor Kit
Glass cleaner

If your tile grout is dirty and stained but still sound, consider whitening the grimy grout with colorant. It's an easy, inexpensive four-step process with a DAP Kwik Seal Grout Recolor Kit. The kit contains everything you need and covers about 100 sq. ft. of 4-in. tile (smaller tile will have more grout lines and require more material).

1. Sponge on the pre-treat solution and let it sit for five minutes. Then scrub the grout with the supplied brush. Wipe clean with the chamois.

1

2. Apply colorant. Squirt a thin bead of the Color+Seal coating on the grout lines in a 2-sq.-ft. section. Then scrub the colorant with the grout brush included in the kit.

3. Remove excess colorant. Wipe the excess colorant from the tile using the chamois. Wipe only the tile, not the grout lines. Let dry for 30 minutes.

4. Buff to remove haze. Apply a light mist of glass cleaner and buff the tile with a clean rag or chamois. Let dry for a full 24 hours before exposing it to water.

How to wash windows

PROFESSIONAL
COST: $266

YOUR COST: $25

SAVINGS: $241

COMPLEXITY
Simple

TOOLS
10- or 12-in.
  squeegee
Replacement blades
  (rubbers)
Scrubber

MATERIALS
Bucket
Hand dishwashing
  liquid
Lint-free rags or
  small towels

Wash your windows the fastest way with crystal-clear, streak-free results. The keys to success are buying a good squeegee and keeping it fitted with a sharp, new rubber blade. A high-quality squeegee will have a metal frame and a replaceable rubber blade. The same high-quality window washing tools the pros use are readily available at home centers and full-service hardware stores.

You don't need fancy buckets or special soap. Any large bucket will do. Just add a couple of gallons of water and about a teaspoon of dishwashing liquid and you're ready to go. In warm weather, you'll get a little more working time by using cool water. If you've procrastinated so long that you're washing windows in below-freezing temps, add windshield washing solution until the water doesn't freeze on the glass.

Scrubber or sponge? It's up to you. A scrubber works great and is worth buying if you have a lot of medium to large panes of glass. But a good-quality sponge is all you really need, especially if most of your windowpanes are small.

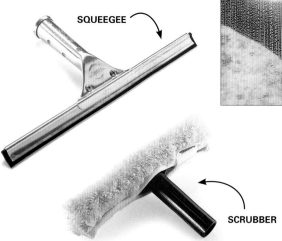

SQUEEGEE

SCRUBBER

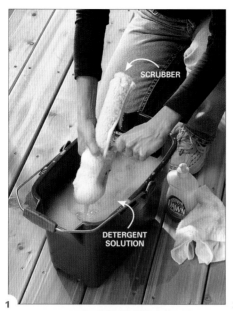

1. Dip the scrubber in a solution of 1 teaspoon dishwashing liquid to two gallons of water. Squeeze excess water from the scrubber.

2. Scrub the glass, working at all angles to clean the edges. Make sure to cover every square inch of the glass.

3. Tip the squeegee so that only the corner contacts the glass. Then, starting at the top corner of the glass, clean a narrow strip of glass from top to bottom on one side. This clean strip makes it easier to start the horizontal strokes.

"Fanning" techniques used by pros take practice to master. Instead, the method we show allows you to get great results immediately. We're moving the squeegee horizontally across the glass (Photos 4 – 6), but vertical strokes will work too. If you work vertically, angle the squeegee to direct excess water toward the uncleaned area.

NARROW CLEAN STRIP

4

SQUEEGEE

LINT-FREE RAG

5

2" OVERLAP

ANGLE SQUEEGEE

6

WIPE PERIMETER

MICROFIBER RAG

7

4. Squeegee across the top. Press the squeegee blade against the glass in the upper corner and pull it steadily across the window. Concentrate on keeping the top of the squeegee in contact with the top edge of the window.

5. Wipe the blade of the squeegee on the clean towel in your front pocket or wipe it across the scrubber to remove dirt and excess water.

6. Work down the window. Begin again, with the top of the squeegee overlapping the previous stroke about 2 in. Pull the squeegee across the window at an angle to direct excess water down. Wipe and repeat.

7. Use the rag in your pocket to wipe up excess water along the bottom edge of the window. Then poke your finger into a dry spot on a separate lint-free rag and run it around the perimeter of the window to remove any remaining suds. Wipe off any streaks using a clean area of the lint-free rag. Change rags when you can't find any fresh, clean areas.

pro tips!

➤ Microfiber rags work great for window cleaning. They're available in the cleaning section of some home centers and hardware stores.

8

8. **You can use a squeegee inside the house, too**. Wash divided-light windows with a sponge and a small squeegee. If you can't find a small enough squeegee, you can cut off a larger one to fit your glass size. Scrub the glass with a wrung-out sponge. The key is to squeeze most of the soapy water out of the sponge to eliminate excessive dripping and running. Then use the tip of the squeegee to clear a narrow strip at the top (same technique as Photo 3). Pull the squeegee down and wipe the perimeter. Keep a rag in your pocket to wipe the squeegee and quickly clean up soapy water that runs onto the woodwork. Use a separate clean rag to wipe the perimeter of the glass. New microfiber rags (Photo 7) work great for window cleaning.

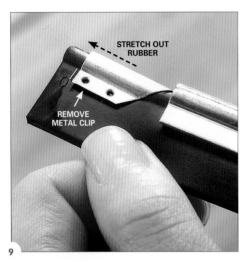

STRETCH OUT RUBBER

REMOVE METAL CLIP

9

How to change your squeegee blade

9. To remove the old blade, grab the end of the blade and stretch it out to expose the metal clip. Slide the clip off. Then slide the blade out the opposite end. Blades without clips are held by screws and the clamp on the handle.

10. Install the new blade. Slide the new blade into the metal channel. Stretch it as in Photo 10 and reinstall the metal clip. If necessary, cut the end of the blade to leave 1/8 to 3/16 in. protruding from the channel.

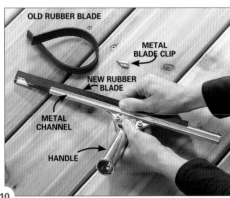

OLD RUBBER BLADE

METAL BLADE CLIP

NEW RUBBER BLADE

METAL CHANNEL

HANDLE

10

pro tips!

➤ Buy a good squeegee and replace the blade frequently. Look for replacement blades, also called rubbers, where you buy the squeegee and pick up two or three to have on hand.

The pros we talked to change their squeegee blades as often as once a day. That's because you just can't do a good job if the edge of the blade becomes nicked, sliced or rounded over with use.

If your squeegee leaves streaks or just isn't performing like new, don't hesitate to replace the blade. You can get a little more mileage out of blades that aren't nicked or sliced by simply reversing them to expose a fresh edge. When you store the squeegee, make sure nothing touches the blade.

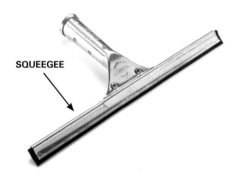

SQUEEGEE

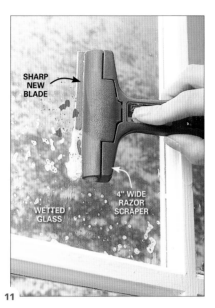

SHARP
NEW
BLADE

4" WIDE
RAZOR
SCRAPER

WETTED
GLASS

11

Tips for hard-to-clean windows

11. The razor blade solution: Remove paint specks and labels with a razor blade mounted in a holder. Always use a new blade to avoid scratching the glass. Wet the window first and push the blade across once. Rinse the blade and repeat on the next section to avoid trapping debris under the blade that could scratch the glass. Don't use a razor blade on tempered glass.

pro tips!

Dried paint, sticky labels, tree pitch and bug crud may not yield to plain soap and water. Here are a few tips for removing this tough grime.

➤ Scrape wetted glass with a new, sharp razor blade to remove dried paint (Photo 11).

➤ Remove tree pitch or bug droppings with a fine white nylon scrub pad. Wet the glass first and rub in an inconspicuous area to make sure you're not scratching the glass.

➤ Add 1/2 cup of ammonia per gallon of water to help remove greasy dirt.

➤ Loosen sticky residue left from labels or tape by soaking it with a specialty product like Goof Off. You'll find Goof Off in the paint department at hardware stores and home centers. Then scrape off the residue with a razor blade.

Chapter 8

Exterior

Stop invasive plants from taking over your garden

Many plants multiply by dropping seeds and by sending out roots that establish new plants. A layer of mulch will prevent the seeds from taking root. But to stop those aggressive roots, you need a solid barrier. Replant the spreading plants inside underground "collars." The plastic collars should extend at least 10 in. below ground to prevent the roots from sneaking under them. Note: This trick won't work with plants such as strawberries or mint that spread above ground.

1. Slice out the bottom of a 10 in. deep (min.) plastic container with a utility knife.

2. Push this "collar" into the soil (or drive it down with a mallet) to encircle the plant and its invasive root system. If the soil has become compacted, cut around the plant with a spade first.

1

2

Help for root-bound plants

If you buy potted plants or shrubs, they may well be root-bound. With nowhere else to grow, roots form tight circles inside the pot. As the plant grows, the tightly wound roots prevent water and nutrients from reaching the leaves.

1. Before planting, gently coax these roots outward with your fingers.

2. If the roots are very stubborn, make three or four vertical cuts in the root-ball with a sharp knife. Once planted, water often to help the plant get established.

2

PROFESSIONAL COST: $45

YOUR COST: $0

SAVINGS: $45

COMPLEXITY
Simple

TOOLS
Utility knife

MATERIALS
Gloves

Munch-proof your flower bulbs

Keep hungry critters from snacking on your freshly planted flower bulbs.

PROFESSIONAL
COST: $90

YOUR COST: $25

SAVINGS: $65

COMPLEXITY
Simple

TOOLS
Wire cutters

MATERIALS
Gloves
Poultry netting
Wire staple stakes

POULTRY NETTING

TENT STAKES

1

1. After planting, stake poultry netting over the bed. You can either remove the cloth in the early spring or let plants grow through the holes and leave it throughout the growing season.

2. If you want to hide it, just cover with soil or a light layer of mulch.

   It is a good idea to clean up the planting site when you are finished, because any bulb debris—like the papery tunics that fall off the bulbs—can attract the squirrels.

pro tips!

➤ Keep a scrapbook of plant data. Store plant tags and sticks inside a cheap photo album. You can add details such as when and where the plants were purchased, special care or even the plant's location on a sketch of your yard.

Lighten those heavy pots

A simple solution to lighten large pots and create proper drainage.

1. Fill the pot one-third to one-half full with foam packing peanuts. They not only make the pot lighter but also provide space for drainage.

2. Fit a round piece of landscape fabric between the soil and the foam to keep the materials separate. You can use a light potting mix that contains plenty of vermiculite and peat moss to make the pot even lighter. Some packing peanuts dissolve in water; be sure to test yours before putting them in the pot.

PROFESSIONAL COST: $55

YOUR COST: $9

SAVINGS: $46

COMPLEXITY
Simple

TOOLS
Scissors

MATERIALS
Foam packing peanuts
Landscape fabric
Potting mix

LIGHTWEIGHT POTTING MIX

LANDSCAPE FABRIC

FOAM PACKING PEANUTS

pro tips!

Watering tips for a lush lawn

Proper watering is the single most important thing you can do to keep your lawn in tip-top shape. And even though lawn watering is pretty simple, there are tricks and tips that can help you save time and money. Here are some of our best tips for watering quickly and efficiently to maintain a strong lawn.

Watering wisdom

➤ **Adjust your watering to the conditions.** Different areas of your lawn will have different watering requirements. The key is to make note of this as you water so you can tailor your watering. For example, south-facing hills may require more water; areas under trees, less.

➤ **Keep watering in a drought.** Don't believe the common wisdom that grass goes dormant in a drought. If you don't provide your grass some moisture in a drought, it will die.

➤ **Water in the morning if possible.** The grass can benefit from the water all day long. Plus, watering in the evening may encourage the growth of harmful fungi.

Buy an impact sprinkler on a tripod

➤ **Impact sprinklers are even more versatile if you buy one that's attached to a tripod.** These are great for large areas because the extra height increases the distance the sprinkler will throw water. There are other benefits too. You can easily adjust the spray pattern with less stooping, and you can direct the spray over the top of bushes and flower gardens. And finally, the adjustable legs allow you to level out the sprinkler on uneven ground. Look for tripod impact sprinklers at home centers and garden centers.

Using well water? Run all your sprinklers at once

➤ **Constant starting and stopping will prematurely wear out your well pump.** If you're using a well to provide water for your lawn, try to connect as many sprinklers as possible to maximize water flow. This will keep the well pump running continuously and increase its life span.

Add a remote hose connection for easier watering

➤ If you're constantly dragging long lengths of hose from the house to the far corners of your yard, consider a hose connection. Depending on how much time and expense you want to put into it, this can be as simple as a length of garden hose connected to a fence with pipe straps, or an underground pipe complete with a vacuum breaker at the house. Either way, you'll save a ton of time and effort by not having to deal with long hoses.

Check soil moisture to determine watering time

➤ Common wisdom for establishing the correct length of time to water is to place a pie pan in the yard and note how long it takes to fill 1/2 in. deep. But the expert we talked to prefers a more accurate method that takes soil conditions into account. Heavier soil doesn't absorb moisture nearly as fast as loose or sandy soil, so it needs to be watered longer.

After an extended warm, dry period (dry soil is the key) set up your sprinkler and set a timer for 30 minutes. Then turn off the water and check the soil for moisture depth. Do this by pushing a shovel into the lawn and tipping it forward to expose the soil. See how deep the water has penetrated. Moist soil will be darker. Your goal is to run the sprinkler until the water penetrates 3 to 4 in. into the soil.

If the water has not penetrated far enough, restart the watering and continue to keep track of the time. Check again in another 15 minutes. With trial and error, you'll eventually arrive at the optimal length of time to water for your soil type and water pressure.

pro tips! *Watering tips for a lush lawn*

Water in the fall

➤ **Your lawn still needs water in autumn, even though the leaves are changing, the growing season is winding down and your grass isn't growing fast.** Fall watering helps your lawn recover from summer stress and gain strength for the winter ahead. Also, if you fertilize in the fall, watering is necessary for the fertilizer to dissolve and soak into the ground where it's needed. So don't put your hoses or sprinklers away until the ground starts to freeze.

Water grass seed carefully

➤ **Seeding is a great way to grow a lawn or patch a bare spot.** The key to success is proper watering. For seeds to germinate and grow, they must be kept constantly damp until the seedlings establish roots. Once the seeds sprout, a dry period of even a day will likely kill the new sprouts, and you'll have to start over.

Seeds covered with fabric or mulch or mixed with a mulch-like product stand a better chance. But even with this protection, you should water lightly at least once or twice a day during hot or windy days. Sprinkle the seeds with a light mist until they sprout. A hard spray or big droplets of water will wash the seeds away or make them clump together. After the seeds sprout, keep watering once a day until the grass is ready for its first mowing.

Choose the best sprinkler for your needs

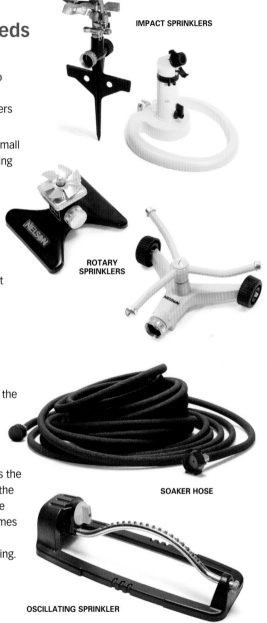

IMPACT SPRINKLERS

ROTARY SPRINKLERS

➤ **Impact sprinklers are a great all-around choice because they're so adjustable and generally waste less water.** But there may be better sprinklers for small, difficult-to-water areas.

Rotary sprinkler If you have just a small circular area to water, the round watering pattern of a rotary sprinkler is perfect.

Soaker hoses Long, narrow spaces like boulevards are easiest to water with flat soaker/sprinkler hoses.

Oscillating sprinkler For square or rectangular areas, it's hard to beat an oscillating sprinkler. It's not the most efficient design, but the spray pattern makes it easy to water all the way into the corners.

➤ **Save water with an impact or rotary sprinkler**

Sprinklers that spray water high into the air or break up water into a mist are very inefficient, especially if you're watering when it's hot and dry. A large percentage of the water will simply evaporate before it ever reaches the grass. Impact and rotary sprinklers, on the other hand, can be adjusted to keep the water nearer the ground; the water comes out in streams or large drops that fall quickly to the ground without evaporating. You'll save water and money using an impact or rotary sprinkler whenever possible.

SOAKER HOSE

OSCILLATING SPRINKLER

Eliminate grubs

PROFESSIONAL COST: $100

YOUR COST: $25

SAVINGS: $75

COMPLEXITY
Simple

TOOLS
Shovel
Broadcast spreader

MATERIALS
Grub insecticide

Grub-chewed turf has patchy areas that wilt and die. You can easily pull up the affected turf if you tug on it. Another indicator of grubs may be increased raccoon, bird or mole activity. They like to dig up and eat the grubs at night. While this may sound good, the moles will kill the grass as they forage for grubs.

Lawn grubs are the larval stage of moths and beetles. The grubs eat the roots of grass, setting them up for death by dehydration.

To remedy, be vigilant. Are beetles swarming around your porch light? In the next month, keep an eye out for patches of grass that wilt or are blue-green on hot days. They may be larvae-infested.

1. Check for grubs. Pierce the lawn with a shovel in a U-shape. Peel back the lawn (as though rolling up a rug) and count the white grubs in a 1-sq.-ft. area.

GRUBS

GRUB

1

2

2. If you count six to 10 grubs (white wormlike larvae with black heads) under a 1-ft.-square area of sod, treat your lawn with a grub insecticide (available at home centers and nurseries). Follow the manufacturer's directions carefuly. Or talk to a professional (search "Grass Service" online) about treating your yard. They will be familiar with the grub problems in your region and the most suitable treatment methods.

3. If you spot the grubs but your count is lower than six per square foot, baby your lawn to strengthen its natural defenses. Mow on higher blade settings and water thoroughly but infrequently to encourage the grass to grow new, deep roots. Do not cut off more than one-third of the grass height at each mowing to avoid stressing the plant.

pro tips!

➤ Moles can eat their weight in worms and grubs every day, so they find healthy, well-watered lawns—which are full of worms and grubs—very attractive. Tunneling as fast as a foot per minute under the sod, one mole can make an average yard look like an army invaded it.

   If you can live with them, they generally won't cause any serious, long-term damage to your yard. However, if you can't, you'll have to trap or remove them. The population density of moles is generally no more than three per acre, so catching even one might take care of the problem.

COMPLEXITY
Simple

TOOLS
Hose
Spade

MATERIALS
Top-soil
Grass seed or yard
  patch mixture or
  sod

Fix dog spots on grass

Dog spots are round patches about 4 to 8 in. in diameter with dead grass in the middle, encircled by dark green grass. They're most apparent in the early spring when dormant grass first begins to turn green again.

Dog urine contains high concentrations of acids, salts and nitrogen, which burn (dry out) the grass roots and kill them. As rain washes the area, the urine is diluted and the nitrogen spreads, causing the grass surrounding the spot to grow faster and turn greener. You have to replant your grass; it won't come back on its own.

1. Soak the patch until the grass is sopping wet to dilute the urine acids and salts and wash them deeper into the soil, beyond the grass roots. Let the hose run for at least three minutes.

DOG URINE SPOT

1

pro tips!

An ounce of prevention

➤ **Soak.** Soak your pet's favorite areas in your lawn to get the salts out of the root zone before they kill the grass.

➤ **Fertilize.** Fertilize your lawn in the spring to boost the overall color and mask the darker-green dog spots.

➤ **Train.** Train your pet to urinate in a designated area. Replace or repair the grass in this area annually or cover it with mulch.

➤ **Hydrate.** Keep your pet well hydrated to make its urine less concentrated.

2

3

2. Scrape up the dead grass with a hand rake and remove it. Rough up the area to loosen the soil 1/2 in. deep. Seeds germinate better in soft soil.

3. Sprinkle on a 1/2-in.-thick layer of topsoil, then pepper it with grass seed, or use a commercial yard patch mixture (available at most nurseries or home centers) or even sod. In any case, the secret of good germination is keeping the seed moist until the new grass is about 3 in. high.

4. When you're watering new seed, moisten the soil daily and keep it damp—but don't soak it. Overwatering is a common mistake. Growth should take four to six weeks.

Create a clean garden bed edge

PROFESSIONAL
COST: $240

YOUR COST: $62

SAVINGS: $178

COMPLEXITY
Simple

TOOLS
Square spade
Hacksaw
Shovel

MATERIALS
Gloves
String
Aluminum edging
File
Stakes

CAUTION:
Call your local utilities or 811 to locate underground lines before you dig and install all edging.

The simplest and most subtle borders that effectively separate your lawn from garden are 4-in.-deep strips of steel, aluminum or plastic. They all bend easily into smooth, graceful curves and stop the spread of grass roots. However, painted aluminum and steel offer the sleekest, most refined look because they almost disappear against the grass and garden bed. The plastic types have a prominent black bulge along the top edge. All work best on fairly even terrain.

We chose aluminum because it was much lighter. You get a professional look without the heavy lifting and it won't rust!

Plan to set the border with the top edge about 1/2 in. above the soil level to maintain the lawn/garden separation and keep roots from crossing over the top. This makes the border almost invisible and allows you to mow right over the top.

1. Cut a narrow, 4-in.-deep trench with one vertical side along the lawn edge. Shave the vertical edge to smooth out curves. Follow a string line for straight edges.

2. Snap together the 8-ft. border sections, drop the edging into the trench and lay it against the vertical edge. Cut the final section to length with a hacksaw.
   Be aware that the thin top edge can hurt bare feet. After cutting it, make sure you round off any sharp edges with a file.

ALUMINUM EDGING

SQUARE SPADE

1

INTERLOCKING JOINT

2

pro tips!

➤ The key to setting this border is to cut a clean vertical edge along the grass with a square spade (Photo 1). Then you can lay the border tightly against the edge when you stake and backfill it. Simply follow the edges of your lawn, making smooth, gradual curves. To make smooth, sharp curves, bend the edging around a circular form.

3. Support the edging with stakes. Drive the stakes to set the depth at about 1/2 in. above the soil level of the lawn. If the edging drops too low, pry it up with the tip of your shovel. This makes the border almost invisible and allows you to mow right over the top.

4. Backfill along the edging with soil from the garden bed and compress it firmly. Leave room on top for mulch.

5. The end result is a clean strip that subtly separates the lawn from the garden.

pro tips!

➤ Steel edging is the most common metal edging, although you might not find it at local nurseries. Look for it at larger garden centers or at landscape suppliers, which is where most pros get it. (Search "Landscape Equipment and Supplies" online or in your Yellow Pages.) Steel edging comes in 4-in.-wide by 10-ft.-long strips in a variety of colors. Keep in mind that it'll eventually rust, especially in a salt environment. It's heavy, floppy stuff and needs almost full support when you transport it.

➤ Aluminum edging, besides being lighter and stiffer, won't rust and is also available in a wide variety of colors. Look for it through landscaping suppliers, although it might be difficult to find. You might have to order it. Be sure stakes are included with your purchase.

➤ You'll find black plastic edging at every garden center and home center, sometimes in both regular and heavy-duty thicknesses. Buy the thicker material. It better withstands those inevitable bumps and hard knocks that go with lawn mowing.

PROFESSIONAL
COST: $35

YOUR COST: $15

SAVINGS: $20

COMPLEXITY
Simple

TOOLS
Socket/ratchet set

MATERIALS
Replacement trimmer
head and string

Install a simpler weed trimmer head

If you've ever struggled to replace or pull out a string trimmer line, you'll love this fix!

The frustrating old trimmer head can be replaced with an easy-loading version (adapter required for some models). Echo Inc. (echo-usa.com) produces a universal trimmer head with a string-loading system so simple your kindergartner could figure it out. Short pieces of string line are pushed into the trimmer head, and a locking system catches the line like a fish on a hook. To change the line, simply pull it through the cutter head and push in a new piece.

Photos 2 and 3 show how to mount the replacement head on machines with threaded shafts. Before mounting the new head, determine which triangular adapter piece and retaining nut fit the threaded shaft.

1. **Remove the trimmer head.** Remove the spool of line from the trimmer housing. The most common method is to push in, twist and pull off the spool. If your trimmer head differs, follow the manufacturer's instructions to remove the old head. The head is attached to the trimmer with a retaining nut or bolt. Ratchet it free and pull it off (some nuts and bolts will be reverse-threaded).

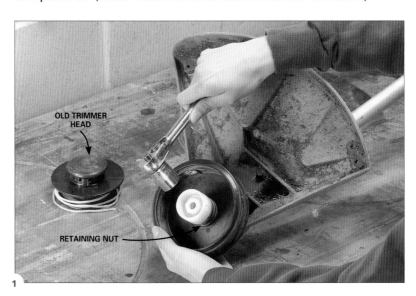

OLD TRIMMER HEAD

RETAINING NUT

1

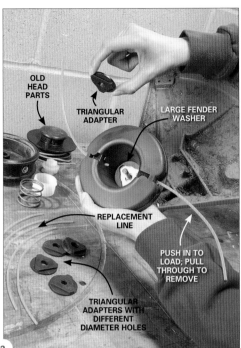

OLD HEAD PARTS

TRIANGULAR ADAPTER

LARGE FENDER WASHER

REPLACEMENT LINE

PUSH IN TO LOAD; PULL THROUGH TO REMOVE

TRIANGULAR ADAPTERS WITH DIFFERENT DIAMETER HOLES

2

2. **Slide on the new head.** Slip the large fender washer over the threaded shaft and the new trimmer head over the washer. Slide the triangular adapter piece onto the shaft and align with the triangular recess in the trimmer head.

3. **Fasten the head.** Slide the small fender washer over the triangular adapter piece, attach the retaining nut and tighten it securely.

CORRECT RETAINING NUT

SMALL FENDER WASHER

NUTS AND BOLTS FOR OTHER BRANDS

3

Protect outdoor furniture

**PROFESSIONAL
COST: $100**

YOUR COST: $20

SAVINGS: $80

COMPLEXITY
Simple

MATERIALS
Drop cloth
Safety glasses
Gloves
Several disposable
  containers
Epoxy, clear-coated
  for wood
Glossy spar varnish
Several natural-
  bristle brushes
China-bristle brush
120-grit sandpaper
220-grit sandpaper

pro tips!

➤ **Two-part
epoxy.** Mix
the resin and
hardener
thoroughly in a
clean, disposable
container, in
the proportions
specified by the
manufacturer.

If you'd like to preserve the natural wood appearance of your outdoor furniture or your wood entry door, take a lesson from boat builders. Boat builders and restorers use multiple coats of epoxy and spar varnish to protect wood—instead of spar varnish alone—because the combination is much stronger than either finish is separately. Epoxy creates a tough, flexible moisture barrier; spar varnish adds depth and UV protection, which keeps the epoxy from yellowing and eventually disintegrating.

The epoxy, a special type for clear-coating wood, is sold at woodworking suppliers, hobby shops and marine supply stores, or go online. It's expensive, but when fully cured, the finish is very tough and will last for years.

1. Sand and clean the wood, then stain it if desired. Mix the epoxy resin and hardener thoroughly in a disposable container. A batch will start to harden in about 30 minutes, faster if it's hot out, so just mix a small quantity the first time to see how far you get. Apply the epoxy with an inexpensive natural-bristle brush. Spread the epoxy, then lightly drag the brush back through to even it out and eliminate bubbles. Work quickly and allow the thick epoxy to flatten without brushing it too much. You'll need a new brush for each coat. When the epoxy in the container starts to stiffen and feel warm, discard the container and the brush and mix a new batch.

Allow to harden overnight, then sand thoroughly with 120-grit sandpaper to flatten out any ridges and flaws and apply another coat. The manufacturer recommends three coats.

NATURAL-BRISTLE BRUSH

EPOXY

1

UNSANDED EPOXY

2. Sand the final coat of epoxy after it has cured for at least 24 hours with 220-grit to create a smooth, scratch-free surface for the varnish. Then vacuum the surface and wipe it with a damp rag.

GLOSSY SPAR VARNISH

CHINA-BRISTLE BRUSH

3. Apply three coats of oil-based exterior glossy spar varnish. with a high-quality china-bristle brush, brushing with the grain. Sand the varnish between coats. Add coats of varnish every few years to keep the finish looking fresh.

PROFESSIONAL
COST: $75

YOUR COST: $0

SAVINGS: $75

COMPLEXITY
Simple

TOOLS
Diagonal cutter
Cat's paw
Hammer or pry bar
Corded drill
Drill bit set

MATERIALS
Shim or very thin
  wood blocks
2-1/2 in. deck screws

Replace loose, popped deck nails

Decking swells and shrinks as it goes through repeated cycles of wet and dry seasons. This frequently causes nails to loosen and pop up above the deck boards. You can drive them down again, but chances are that's only a short-term solution. They'll probably pop up again. The long-term solution is to remove the popped nails and replace them with deck screws.

The trick is to pull the old nails without marring the decking. Always use a block under your prying tool. And work on tough-to-get-out nails using several steps. A diagonal cutter works well for nails that only protrude slightly (Photo 1). The slim jaws can slip under the head. You'll only raise the nail a slight amount, so you may have to repeat this process two or three times. Once the nailhead is high enough, you can grip it with a cat's paw or hammer claw without marring the deck board (Photo 2). Be sure to use thin wood shims to protect the decking.

1. Start with a diagonal cutter. Grab slightly protruding nails directly under the head with a diagonal cutter. Roll the cutter back onto shim to pry the nail up slightly.

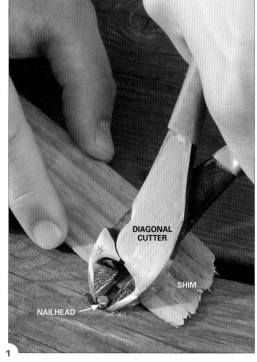

DIAGONAL CUTTER

SHIM

NAILHEAD

1

SHIM

NAILHEAD

CAT'S PAW

NAILHEAD

2

DECK SCREW SET FLUSH

3

2. Yank the nail with cat's paw. Tap the claw of a cat's paw under the nailhead and lever the nail up. Finish pulling with a hammer or pry bar. Again, protect the deck board with a shim or thin block.

NAILHEAD

3. Replace the nail with a screw. There's no need to drill a pilot hole if you send the screw down the old nail hole. (One drawback of screws is that their heads are larger than nailheads and can be unsightly. We recommend that you buy deck screws in a color that most closely matches the aged decking.) Stand on the deck board to hold it down. Then drive a 2-1/2 in. deck screw down into the old nail hole. Set the screwhead flush to the surface.

4. Minor dents will disappear when the wood swells after the next rain.

pro tips!

Solutions for stubborn nails

➤ **If the head breaks off a stubborn nail and you can't get it with a pry bar, try pulling it with locking pliers.** Grip the nail tip and roll the pliers over to get it going.

➤ **If the nail shank breaks off, don't worry.** Just drill a pilot hole beside the nail and drive a screw. The screwhead will cover the nail.

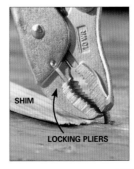

SHIM

LOCKING PLIERS

SCREWHEAD

BROKEN NAIL

Patch leaky gutters

Gutter leaks usually start at rusty spots or seams that have opened up because of expansion and contraction. If your gutter is still basically sound, the easiest way to stop the leak is by covering the damaged area with roof and gutter repair tape.

COMPLEXITY
Simple

TOOLS
Stiff scraper
Wire brush
Scissors or razor
  knife

MATERIALS
Roof and gutter
  repair tape
Special adhesive
  primer (if required)

> **CAUTION:**
> Make sure ladder
> is secure.

1. Prepare the gutter by scraping out as much old tar or caulk as possible. Clean the area around the leak with a stiff scraper and a wire brush, then rinse off all dust and wipe completely dry to give the tape a clean surface for bonding.

  If the gutter is badly rusted or has been heavily coated with tar that you can't scrape out, spray on a special adhesive primer before applying the tape.

OLD TAR

LEAKY SEAM

1

GUTTER TAPE

2

2. Cut the gutter repair tape with a scissors or a razor knife long enough to overlap the leaky area by at least 6 in. in each direction.

3. Tear the paper backing off the tape and lightly adhere one edge of the tape to the top of the gutter. Starting at the center, press tape firmly into place. Follow the contours of the gutter and smooth out all the wrinkles and bubbles. Overlap long seams by at least 1 in. and end seams by 4 in.

1" MINIMUM OVERLAP

3

Reattach loose vinyl siding

PROFESSIONAL COST: $100

YOUR COST: $10

SAVINGS: $90

COMPLEXITY
Simple

TOOLS
Pry bar

MATERIALS
Siding removal tool
  or zip tool

Vinyl siding is installed by interlocking the top and bottom edges of the panels. Properly installed, the panels should stay permanently locked together. If you have panels that have separated from poor installation, impact damage or severe weather, first check for clues that the siding was improperly installed. The installer may have tried to straighten unlevel courses by pulling the panels up taut, or pressing them down, then nailing them. Or perhaps the nails weren't driven straight and level, resulting in panels that later buckled.

Vinyl siding panels may come undone because these problems—or repeated temperature changes—allow the panels to expand, contract and loosen.

1. Buy a siding removal tool at a home center or a siding retailer. This tool can be used for vinyl, aluminum or steel siding. The hook on the tool grabs the locking face under the bottom edge of each panel.

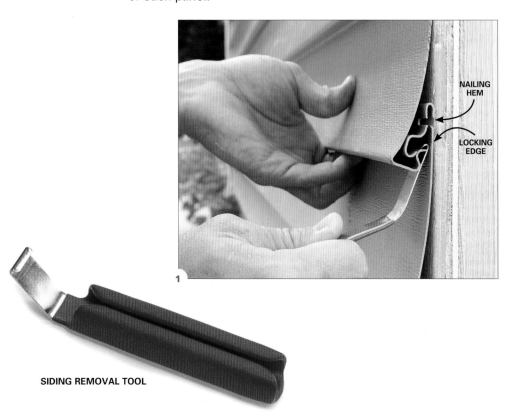

NAILING HEM

LOCKING EDGE

SIDING REMOVAL TOOL

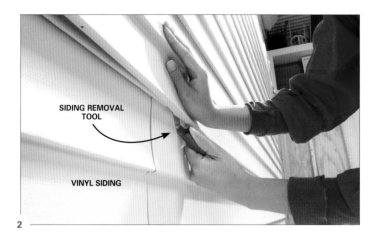

SIDING REMOVAL
TOOL

VINYL SIDING

2

2. To reattach a panel, first use the siding tool to grab the panel's locking edge, then pull down. At the same time, use the heel of your hand to push the panel edge to catch the locking face on the lower siding course. Work the siding tool and heel of your hand along the edge of the loosened panel in this manner until the two courses of vinyl have snapped back together.

3. If it doesn't reattach easily, check the nailing technique on the lower course. If the nails were driven too tight, the nailing flange may be dimpled. Its locking face won't be in a straight-line position to easily receive the next panel. Take a pry bar and carefully work it behind the nailhead. Back the nail out until the dimple is taken out of the nailing

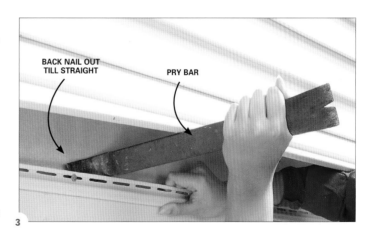

BACK NAIL OUT
TILL STRAIGHT

PRY BAR

3

flange. The siding removal tool (shown) is a must for both removing siding panels and reconnecting them. When you're removing a locked panel, you'll have to wiggle the siding tool as you push it up to successfully grab the locking face's edge.

PROFESSIONAL
COST: $100

YOUR COST: $5

SAVINGS: $95

COMPLEXITY
Simple

TOOLS
Caulk gun
Utility knife

MATERIALS
Color-matched caulk

Patch holes in aluminum and vinyl siding

Nail holes in aluminum and vinyl siding are tough to repair without replacing the entire piece, but a squirt of color-matched caulk from a siding supplier will solve the problem for a lot less money and aggravation.

An easy, nearly-as-good fix that keeps water out and is almost invisible from several feet away is to fill the hole with a color-matched caulk. Home centers don't usually stock it, but siding wholesalers that sell to contractors carry caulks specifically blended for dozens of different shades of siding. If you know the manufacturer and color name of your siding, you can get the exact blend developed for that shade. Otherwise, bring a sample piece or take a photo and ask a salesperson to help you match it.

1. Find caulk colors to match dozens of different siding colors at suppliers that sell to siding contractors.

2. Before filling the hole, wipe the siding clean. Squirt enough caulk into the hole to fill the area behind the hole. Avoid smearing excess caulk all over the surrounding siding—the less you get on the siding, the less obvious the repair will be.

3. Once the caulk is fully cured (which could be several days, depending on the type), trim it flush with the siding using a straightedge razor blade.

FILL WITH ENOUGH CAULK TO GET BEHIND HOLE

3

COLOR-MATCHED CAULK

Clean vinyl siding

Vinyl siding usually cleans up easily with nothing more than soap and water, and a yearly scrubbing will keep it looking new. If left unchecked, it can cause your home's exterior to look dirty and dingy.

PROFESSIONAL
COST: $250

YOUR COST: $15

SAVINGS: $235

COMPLEXITY
Simple

TOOLS
Bucket
Soft-bristle brush
Sponge
Nylon scrub pad

MATERIALS
General-purpose cleaner
Non-abrasive bathtub cleaner
Ammonia

1. For basic cleaning, use general-purpose cleaner mixed with warm water. Apply it with a soft-bristle cleaning brush, scrubbing the full length of each lap. Start at the bottom to avoid streaking, and use your garden hose to rinse off each section before it dries.

   Mold shows up as black spots on siding, especially in damp and shady areas. You can scrub away the surface mold in a matter of minutes with a 1-to-8 bleach/water solution.

2. For tough spots like paint drips, tar, and pencil and pen marks, use a nonabrasive bathtub cleaner or nylon scrub pad. Use ammonia cleaners or a solution of 1 part bleach in 4 parts water to clean mold and mildew stains. (However, never mix ammonia and bleach.) Rinse thoroughly while the siding is still wet.

   Don't use paint thinner, nail polish remover, spot removers, paint remover, straight chlorine bleach or furniture cleaner on vinyl. These types of cleaners can damage the surface of the siding.

> **CAUTION:**
> Don't use paint thinner, nail polish remover, spot removers, paint remover, straight chlorine bleach or furniture cleaner on vinyl.

> **CAUTION:**
> Don't mix ammonia or any detergent containing ammonia with bleach. The combination forms a poisonous gas.

Easy shingle repair

A broken shingle is both ugly and a leak waiting to happen. But as long as you can find matching shingles (and you're not afraid of heights), the repair is straightforward.

Pick a day when the weather is moderate (between 50 and 70 degrees F) to do the repair—too cold and the shingles can crack; too warm and the shingle sealants are tough to break. Replacing the shingle will only take about 10 minutes—just be careful not to damage any other shingle.

1. Each shingle has an adhesive tar sealant strip down the center that grips the shingle above it. Gently tap a flat bar under the shingles to break the seal-down strips free to get at the nails and get the damaged shingle out. Don't force it—shingles rip easily. Loosen the tabs under the broken shingle and the next two courses above it.

NAIL REMOVAL ZONE

1

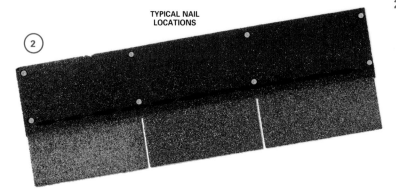

TYPICAL NAIL LOCATIONS

2

2. Shingles are fastened with eight nails each—four at the center just above the tab slots and four through the shingle above it—and you have to lift up all the shingles that cover those nails to remove them.

NAIL

3

EDGE OF NEW SHINGLE

4

3. After all the tabs are loose, wedge the notch of the flat bar up under the damaged shingle to each nail, centering the nail in the flat bar notch. To avoid ripping shingles, gently work the pry bar under both tabs as you push it up.

Pop out the nails by prying underneath the shingle instead of trying to dig the nailhead out from the top of the shingle; that will wreck the shingle. Then push the shingle down from the nailhead and pull out the nail. After removing the center row of nails on the damaged shingle, lift the undamaged shingles above it and remove the next row of nails. Then pull out the damaged shingle.

4. Slide the new shingle up into place. Gently lift the tab of the shingle above, propping the tabs above as you nail to avoid breaking them. Nail the center row first, then the center row of the course above it, nailing 1/2 in. over from the old holes. Nail at the top of the slots between the tabs, just above the sealant strip.

5. Seal the loose shingle tabs to the roof with roof cement and a caulking gun.

pro tips!

➤ If you don't have a few extra shingles stored in the garage or attic, take a scrap of the shingle to a home center or roofing supplier to find a match. You may have to buy a full bundle.

Auto

PROFESSIONAL
COST: $100

YOUR COST: $25

SAVINGS: $75

COMPLEXITY
Simple

TOOLS
4-in-1 screwdriver

Adjustable wrench

Rags

Battery terminal
  cleaner tool

MATERIALS
Protective eye gear

Gloves

Battery terminal
  protective spray

> **CAUTION:**
> Disconnect the
> negative cable first
> and reconnect it
> last.

Car won't start—here's what to do

You turn the key and hear the dreaded "click." Sure, you may need a new battery, starter or alternator. But before you condemn either the battery or the charging system, follow these steps.

Turn on your dome light and turn the key again. If the dome light dims, focus your attention on the battery and its connections. If the dome light doesn't dim, the starter motor isn't drawing power. Have the starter checked by a professional.

Check the battery voltage. Scratch clean contact areas on the battery posts and test the battery voltage with a test meter. A fully charged battery should read 12.7 volts. At 50 percent charge, the voltage drops to 12.1 volts. A low reading can be the result of poor electrical connections, a problem with the charging system or a battery that is at the end of its life.

You can't always see corroded battery and ground connections, so clean all of them (Photos 1–3). Start with the battery terminals. Note: Disconnect the negative cable first and reconnect it last. Then clean the connection between the battery negative cable and the engine.

Finally, clean the connection between the battery negative cable and the body. If the car starts, the problem is solved. If it doesn't, take the car to the shop and explain what tests you've done. Then have the battery and the starting and charging systems checked out.

> **CAUTION:**
> Always wear eye protection and rubber gloves when working
> with a car battery to prevent accidental injury from battery acid.
> And never smoke around them!

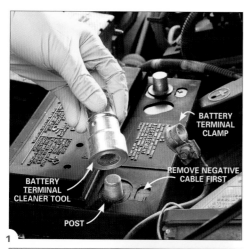

BATTERY TERMINAL CLAMP

REMOVE NEGATIVE CABLE FIRST

BATTERY TERMINAL CLEANER TOOL

POST

1

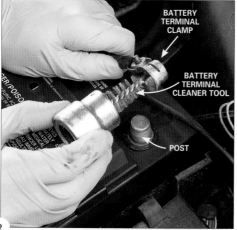

BATTERY TERMINAL CLAMP

BATTERY TERMINAL CLEANER TOOL

POST

2

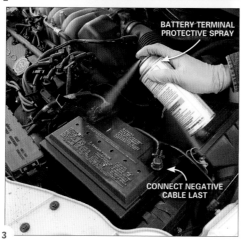

BATTERY TERMINAL PROTECTIVE SPRAY

CONNECT NEGATIVE CABLE LAST

3

1. Check the posts. Disconnect the negative battery terminal and then the positive and use a wire terminal cleaner to clean the posts.

2. Clean the inside of the terminals with the opposite end of the cleaning tool.

3. Protect terminals by applying a light coat of battery terminal protective spray (red).

Replace the 4 most neglected bulbs in your vehicle

Here's how to replace auto light bulbs you never think of until you need them. These are the four most commonly neglected bulbs that can affect your driving experience. Check yours to see if they work, and pick up replacements at any auto parts store.

PROFESSIONAL COST: $50

YOUR COST: $12

SAVINGS: $38

COMPLEXITY
Simple

TOOLS
Flat-blade
 screwdriver or
 small pry bar

MATERIALS
Gloves
Automotive light
 bulbs as required

Map light bulbs

1. Pry off the lens and pull the bulb out of the spring terminals. Snap in a new bulb.

Dome light bulbs

2. Pry off the dome light lens and spread the spring terminals. Drop one side of the "torpedo"-shaped bulb out of the socket and lift the bulb out. Reverse to install.

1

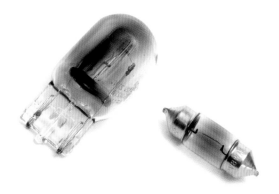

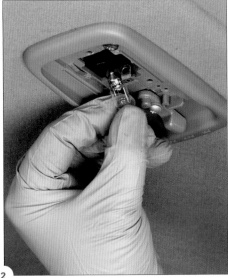

2

High-mount stop bulb

3. A burned-out high-mount stop light bulb can also earn you a ticket. These bulbs are usually replaced from the inside rear windshield. Pry off the interior trim cover. Then rotate the socket a quarter turn and swap out the bulb(s).

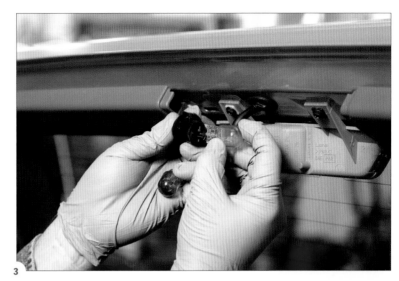

License plate bulb

4. Unscrew the lens or release the locking tab. Twist the bulb socket a quarter turn and pull it out. Push and twist in a new bulb and reinstall. A burned-out license plate bulb can get you a ticket, so replace it if needed.

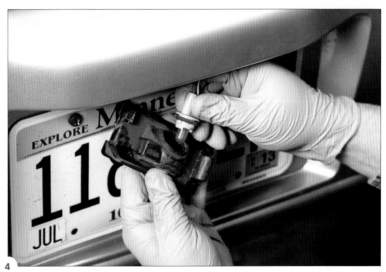

PROFESSIONAL COST: $20

YOUR COST: $0

SAVINGS: $20

COMPLEXITY
Simple

TOOLS
Needle-nose pliers

MATERIALS
Bath towel
Wiper refills

Replace a windshield wiper blade

Stop annoying streaks and chatter from worn wiper blades. Make your car safer. Replace them in minutes.

Your windshield wiper assembly consists of three basic parts: the lower wiper arm that protrudes up from the cowl, the blade that attaches to the wiper arm and the rubber refill that wipes the glass. The thin rubber refill is the part that eventually breaks down from extreme weather conditions, dust and dirt. Most often you can just replace the wiper refill.

However, the blade can also become weak and lose its tension against the glass or even bend slightly from ice and snow. If you have problems with chatter, or if the entire blade isn't making contact with the windshield, replace the entire blade. Both jobs take only a few minutes. It's a good idea to replace the whole blade (sold with refills) every two years.

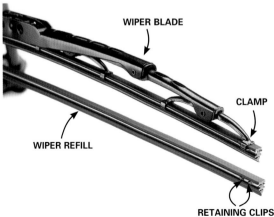

WIPER BLADE

WIPER REFILL

CLAMP

RETAINING CLIPS

pro tips!

➤ Wiper blades should be replaced every six months, especially if you park outside and you live in the desert or in other dusty conditions.

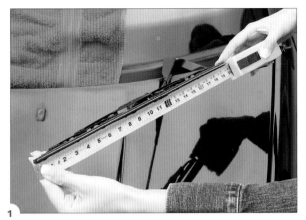

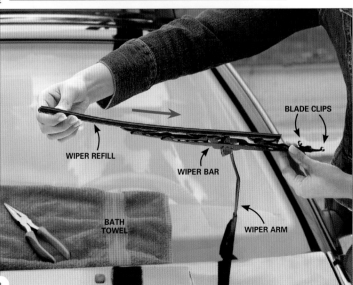

1. Pull the wiper arm back from the glass, then double up a bath towel over your windshield just in case the wiper arm snaps back against the glass. Then measure your wiper blade to get the exact replacement length. Measure both blades and buy refills the exact lengths. Don't assume the refill inserts are the same length on the driver's side and the passenger's side. One is often an inch or more longer than the other.

2. Once the arm is pulled back, pivot the blade so the bottom of the blade flips up toward the top. Locate the small shiny retaining clips near the end of the refill. Pinch them together with a needle-nose pliers and start sliding out the refill. Once the clips slide under the blade clamp, set the pliers down and pull out the old refill with one hand while supporting the blade with the other.

3. Carefully slide the new refill into the same end you pulled the old one from. Make sure the new refill is held between each clamp (to avoid scratching your windshield) and that the retaining clip clicks into position in the last clamp. Gently pivot the arm back into position, release the arm and repeat the process for the other side.

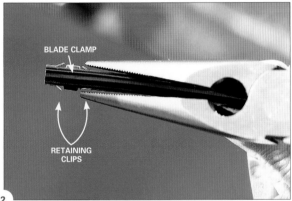

BLADE CLAMP

RETAINING CLIPS

WIPER REFILL

WIPER BAR

BATH TOWEL

WIPER ARM

BLADE CLIPS

Windshield wiper arm replacement

Do your windshield wipers leave unwiped spots for no apparent reason, even after you replaced the blades?

All wiper arms have a hinge at the base that allows the arm to flex as it follows the curvature of the window. If the wiper skips over certain spots, even with a new blade, chances are the hinge is binding from corrosion. It's most common on rear window wipers since they're used less often.

You can oil the hinge, but that's just a temporary fix—the corrosion and binding usually return. To fix the problem permanently, replace the wiper arm (available at an auto parts store).

1. All wiper arms fit onto a splined shaft.

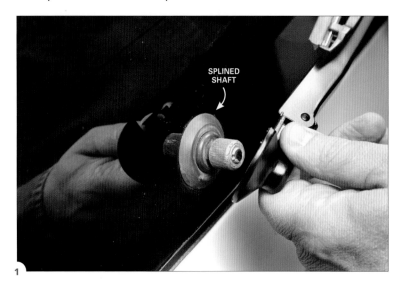

SPLINED SHAFT

2. Some wipers are held with a retaining nut. To replace, lift the plastic protective cover and remove the retaining nut. Then pull the arm off the splined shaft.

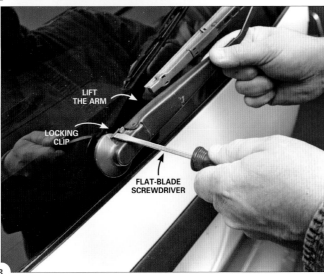

LIFT
THE ARM

LOCKING
CLIP

FLAT-BLADE
SCREWDRIVER

3. Other wipers have a locking clip. Lift the wiper arm a few inches off the glass and slide the locking clip out. Then lower the arm and pull it off the splined shaft.

How to fix a leaking sunroof

PROFESSIONAL
COST: $100

YOUR COST: $10

SAVINGS: $90

COMPLEXITY
Simple

TOOLS
Shop vacuum

MATERIALS
PVC trap adapter, to
  fit vacuum hose
PVC cap, to fit
  adapter
PVC barbed adapter,
  3/8-in.
Vinyl hose, to fit
  barbed adapter
Speedometer cable

You've got water on your seats right below the sunroof, and you're about to take matters into your own hands. We're warning you: Put down the caulk gun and step away from the vehicle. Usually it's simply a drain tube that's clogged with debris. Then the water can't drain and it overflows into the cabin. And that's a simple DIY repair that you can do in about 20 minutes.

Open your sunroof and look for the drain holes in both front corners. Those tubes run through the door pillars and drain through to the rocker panels. You may be tempted to run a coat hanger down the tubes or blast them with compressed air. Don't! You might poke the wire right through the tubing or disconnect it from the drain hole. Then you'd have to remove the entire headliner to reconnect it—a big job. Instead, use a shop vacuum and small-diameter vinyl tubing to suck out the clog (see Photo 1).

If that doesn't do the trick, try running a very small flexible "plumbing" snake down the tube to break up the clog. (Actually, it's a speedometer cable found at any auto parts store for about $8.)

1. Make a hose reducer with ordinary PVC plumbing parts and attach a vinyl hose to the end. Then vacuum the crud out of the water channel and the drain tube.

2. Snake out a really stubborn clog with a speedometer cable. Twist the cable as you feed it down the tube.

VACUUM OUT DRAIN HOLE WITH ATTACHMENT

1

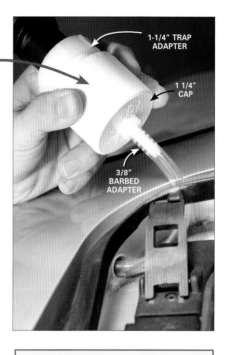

1-1/4" TRAP ADAPTER

1 1/4" CAP

3/8" BARBED ADAPTER

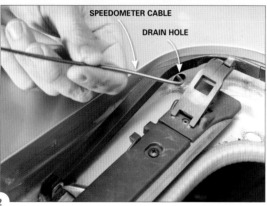

SPEEDOMETER CABLE

DRAIN HOLE

2

CAUTION:
If cleaning the tubes doesn't work, don't try to disassemble the mechanism or bend the sheet metal to get a better fit. That's a job for a top-notch body shop.

Replace the gas lift on your car's hood

PROFESSIONAL COST: $100

YOUR COST: $50

SAVINGS: $50

COMPLEXITY
Simple

TOOLS
Socket/ratchet set
Small flat-blade
 screwdriver
Lift support clamp

MATERIALS
Gas lifts

Gas lifts that hold up car hoods, trunks and rear hatches can wear out and become a problem, especially in cold weather. Why risk injury from a falling hatch? Here's how to fix the problem quickly and cheaply.

Buy a pair of gas lifts (always replace them as a pair) at an auto parts store. They cost $16 to $25 each. Right- and left-side lifts often differ only in very subtle ways, so before you leave the parts store, ask the clerk to label them. Labeling will save you time and frustration when you get home.

The lifts attach to the hood and fender with bolts or a ball and socket arrangement. The bolt styles are easy to identify. Just remove the bolts and replace the lift. The ball and socket styles have a "C"-shaped clip that prevents the socket from popping off the ball. To remove the ends from the ball studs, just insert a small flat-blade screwdriver into the center of the clip to pry it out. That'll allow you to disengage the ball and socket. Use the screwdriver to pry out the C-clip on the replacement lift and snap the end onto the ball.

CAUTION:
Don't rely on a 2x4 to hold the hatch open—it's not a safe alternative.

1. Support the hatch. Lift the hatch slightly higher than its normal open position and have a friend hold the hatch up while you remove the gas lift. Or lock the hatch in place with a lift support clamp attached to the lift shaft while you work on the opposite lift.

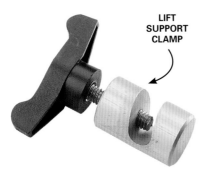

LIFT SUPPORT CLAMP

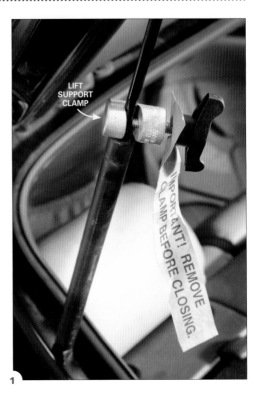

LIFT SUPPORT CLAMP

IMPORTANT! REMOVE CLAMP BEFORE CLOSING.

1

2

2. Disengage the lift. Remove the top portion of the gas lift first. Jam a flat-blade screwdriver into the depression in the center of the C-clamp. (Use a socket and a ratchet to remove the bolted-in-place variety.) Then pull the gas lift off the ball stud. Reverse the procedure to connect the new lift.

A variation on the ball and socket has plastic fingers that snap around the ball. To release the tension on the fingers, pry off the four-legged friction cap and pull the lift off the ball stud.

SOCKET

FRICTION CAP

FRICTION CAP

COMPLEXITY
Simple

MATERIALS
Gloves

Leather/vinyl
repair kit

Patch a tear/hole in leather or vinyl

Learn how to use inexpensive, DIY-friendly repair kits to fix small tears in leather or vinyl car seats before they get big and ugly.

A leather/vinyl repair kit takes only an hour. But don't expect perfection. You'll still see the tear, and you probably won't get a perfect color match. However, this fix will contain the tear and look better than a gaping hole.

You can buy a kit at any hardware store, home center or auto parts store.

1. Follow the cleaning instructions in the kit and trim the damaged area to remove any frayed edges. Then cut the backing fabric so it extends under the tear by at least 1/2 in. Tuck the backing under the damaged area to form a patch. Then apply adhesive around the edges and the middle. Let it dry for the recommended time before adding colorant.

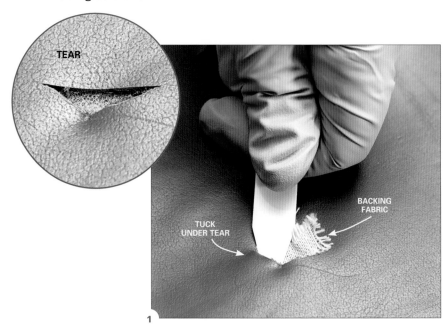

TEAR

TUCK UNDER TEAR

BACKING FABRIC

1

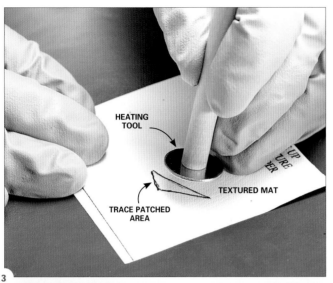

HEATING
TOOL

TEXTURED MAT

TRACE PATCHED
AREA

2. Mix the heat-set colored filler. Take your time and get as close to the color as you can. Apply just enough colorant to fill in the tear.

3. Cover it with the textured mat and apply heat. Touch the heating tool (included with the kit) to the face of a hot clothes iron. Then press the hot tool onto the textured mat (for as long as recommended) and hold it in place. Let it cool.

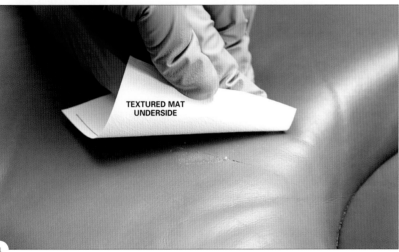

TEXTURED MAT
UNDERSIDE

4. Remove the mat and check out the results. The patch won't be perfect. But it sure beats the look of a tear or burn.

PROFESSIONAL
COST: $150

YOUR COST: $20

SAVINGS: $130

COMPLEXITY
Simple

MATERIALS
Soap

Cotton cloth

Automotive
polishing
compound

Denatured alcohol

Auto body touch-up
paint

How to repair chipped car paint

Remember that gravel truck traveling at 70 mph that suddenly switched lanes in front of you and bounced a few marble-size rocks off your hood? Now you've got several tiny chips in your paint finish that could grow to quarter-size rust spots in a few years. Take care of the problem right away for a few dollars, and you'll save yourself big money later on, not to mention the embarrassment of driving a premature clunker.

At an auto parts store, you'll find a display of auto touch-up paints. Look up your car's year, make and model in the booklet at the display. You'll find a list of factory colors that cars like yours were painted that year. If you have a white vehicle and there is only one white listed for it, just buy that one. If you don't know the color number for your car, you'll have to find it on your vehicle identification plate. This can be challenging. The plate may be located under the hood on the cowl, near the radiator shield or on the jamb of the driver's door. Some owner's manuals will tell you where to look, or a quick call to your dealer will help. Once you find the number, buy a small bottle of touch-up paint. If you can't find the correct color at the display, check with the dealer. Dealers often carry colors for the cars they sell. Also, buy a small can of auto primer.

Now just follow our photo sequence to fix that chip, and remember, don't do this repair in the direct sun or if the temperature is below 50 degrees F.

The fix we show here is for fresh chips that haven't started to rust yet. If you see a rust spot, or have a dent along with your chip, you'll need to do a more challenging fix than we show here. Keep in mind that this repair will be visible under close scrutiny, but if you buy the right touch-up color, it'll be unnoticeable from a few feet away.

CAUTION:
Don't do this repair in the direct sun or if the temperature is below 50 degrees F.

CHIP HAS EXPOSED PRIMER AND METAL BELOW

1

1. This is a typical rock chip that you can fix with this procedure. In fact, even if the chip is about one-fourth the size of a dime, you can still repair it.

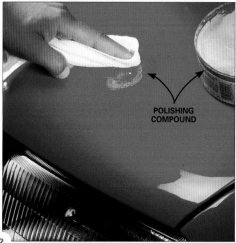

POLISHING COMPOUND

2

2. Clean the chip with soap and water and then dry it with a soft cotton cloth. Rub a dab of automotive polishing compound over the chip to gently soften any ragged edges. Just a dozen swirls or so will do the job. Too much rubbing could damage the clearcoat over the paint and make a cloudy mess.

Denatured Alcohol
Pure
ACE

3

3. Clean the finish with denatured alcohol. Don't flood it with alcohol. Just a few wipes with a soft cloth will do. The alcohol will remove any wax or remaining grime.

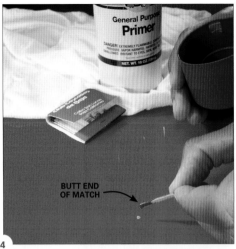

BUTT END
OF MATCH

4

4. Apply a spot of primer with the butt end of a paper match. Fill the area within the chip, just touching the edges of the surrounding paint. Let the primer dry for at least a half hour.

5. Put a small amount of paint over the primer coat. Always test the color on a piece of paper to make sure it matches. The test will also give you a feel for how much paint to load onto the applicator brush. Apply a second coat about one hour later. Let the paint cure for several days and rub it out again gently with polishing compound to feather the edges of the repair.

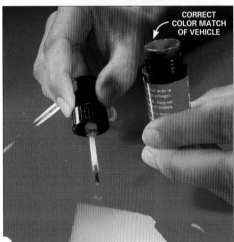

CORRECT
COLOR MATCH
OF VEHICLE

5

pro tips!

➤ If you can only find spray paint with the right color number, you can use it by spraying a bit of paint into the cap and applying it with a fine artist's brush.

PITTED, RUSTY METAL
WITH LOOSE
PAINT EDGE

TOO FAR GONE. This is a chip that should have been repaired long ago. The metal inside the chip has rusted and started to lift the paint at the edges. This fix is less do-it-yourself-friendly and requires sanding, priming and painting.

Winterize car windows and doors

Freezing water can seep into the window tracks and create drag when you try to open the window. That drag can damage the window regulator cables, costing you almost $300. You can avoid the problem entirely by lubricating the window tracks with spray silicone or dry Teflon spray lubricant. Silicone stays slick even in cold weather, so windows slide smoothly, lessening the wear on your window motors.

If water seeps between your door and weather stripping and freezes, you could be frozen out of your car or truck. To prevent the water from freezing you out, coat both the weather stripping and the mating door surfaces with spray silicone.

1. Lower the window and shoot the spray right into the front and back window track. Apply enough lube so it drips all the way down the track.

2. Then operate the window through several open and close cycles to spread the lube along the entire track. Use glass cleaner and a paper towel to remove any spray that lands on the glass.

3. Wipe the silicone lube onto your door and trunk weather stripping. To avoid spraying silicone into your car's interior, spray it directly onto a clean rag.

4. Repeat the procedure on door mating surfaces and the trunk lid.

1

2

PROFESSIONAL
COST: $75

YOUR COST: $30

SAVINGS: $45

COMPLEXITY
Simple

TOOLS
Nail file

Rags

MATERIALS
Graphite lubricant
WD-40
White lithium grease
Silicone spray

> **CAUTION:**
> Don't lubricate
> the gas struts that
> slow the trunk
> movement (you
> could ruin them).

Lubricate car locks, hinges and latches

By the time you start hearing those annoying squeaks and groans whenever you open your door, hood, gas tank lid or trunk, the new-car thrill has probably faded. Recapture some of that new-car feel with a few simple lubricating techniques. With just 10 minutes twice a year, you can quiet those pesky noises and avoid costly repairs.

All you need are a variety of inexpensive lubricants, which will come in handy for household problems as well. White lithium grease is good for metal-to-metal joints like hinges and latches, which need a clinging grease to repel water and hold up under harsh conditions. WD-40 is for light-duty lubrication and freeing up sticking or partially rusted hinges and latches. Silicone spray is great for lubricating nylon, plastic and metal when only a thin layer of lubricant is necessary. And because silicone dries, it won't get clothing greasy. Graphite lubricant is the right choice for locks—it won't attract dirt to fine lock mechanisms like an oil would.

Door locks

1. **Add graphite to door locks**.

We don't think much about our door locks until the key breaks off in the cylinder. Keep these delicate mechanisms moving freely with a blast of dry graphite powder. Push the dust protector flap back slightly with a small metal nail file to get at the lock. A quick pump of the tube will dispense enough graphite. Move the lock cylinder with your key several times to work the graphite into the mechanism. Do this to your trunk lock as well.

1

Hood hinges

2. Lubricate hood hinges.
Wipe the hinge area with a clean rag and spray it with white lithium grease or a few drops of ordinary motor oil. Move the hinge several times to work the grease into the hinge. Be sure to get it into both sides of each hinge. Wipe away the excess to keep it from collecting debris.

Gas tank lid

3. Lubricate the hinge with WD-40.
The gas tank lid really takes abuse, especially in salty environments. Give it a squirt of WD-40 a few times a year to keep it from rusting. Wipe away any excess to keep it from dripping onto your car's finish.

Trunk hinges

4. Lubricate your trunk hinges.
Use the same method you used for the hood hinge. Don't lubricate the gas struts that slow the trunk movement (you could ruin them).

Hood latch

5a. Clean the hood latch.
Wipe away grease, dirt and sand with a clean rag. Try to get any bits of sand that may be embedded in the existing grease.

5b. Spray lubricant and grease on the clean latch.
Spray with WD-40, then move the mechanism several times. Wipe it again and give it a liberal coating of white lithium grease.

5a

5b

Door hinges and latches

6a. Spray door hinges

If the door squeaks every time you open it, the hinges could be bound by corrosion. Spray the hinges with WD-40 to free them, and move the door several times to work in the lubricant. Once the hinges are in working condition, just squirt them with white lithium grease or motor oil, operate the door several times and then wipe any excess away.

6b. Lubricate door latches.

Check the door latch for corrosion. Many door latches now have a nonmetallic composite mechanism, which should be lubricated with a shot of silicone spray.

6a

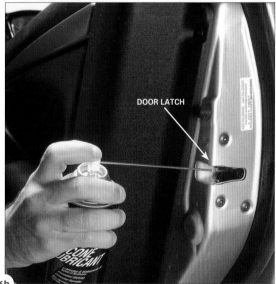

6b

PROFESSIONAL
COST: $100

YOUR COST: $0

SAVINGS: $100

COMPLEXITY
Simple

TOOLS
Digital pressure
 gauge
Tread-depth gauge

Make your tires last

One of the most critical maintenance chores for cars is checking the tires regularly. You'll save hundreds of dollars and extend the life of your tires.

Most drivers ignore their tires until it's too late. Then they have to spend big bucks to replace them. However, you can diagnose tire problems and correct them early by performing three critical maintenance chores: checking the tire pressure, measuring the tread depth regularly and rotating tires every 6,000 miles.

1. All tires lose air, so check your tires every month with a digital pressure gauge. (Digital gauges are easier to read and more accurate than traditional gauges.)

   Always use the same tire pressure gauge and check the air pressure first thing in the morning, not after you've driven on them or they've been sitting in the hot sun.

2. Inflate to the pressures listed on the carmaker's decal (on the driver's door or jamb), NOT the maximum pressure listed on the tire. The recommended tire pressure is based on the weight of your particular vehicle, not the tire brand or tread style. Never assume that the maximum air pressure shown on the tire's sidewall is the same as the recommended tire pressure. Filling to the maximum

CAUTION:
A tire pressure monitoring system measures the tire's pressure and notifies the driver when pressure drops 25 percent below the manufacturer's recommended level, which can be as much as 8 lbs. off.

DIGITAL PRESSURE
GAUGE

①

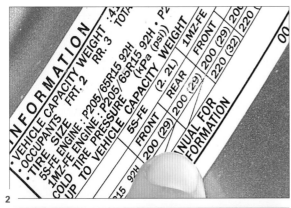

2

3

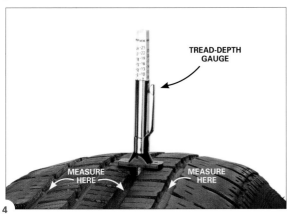

TREAD-DEPTH GAUGE

MEASURE HERE

MEASURE HERE

4

pressure always means you're overinflating your tires.

3. Remove the valve stem cap. Don't lose it—on some sensors the cap is the antenna. Center the gauge over the valve stem and push on it in one quick motion, then release. Press the air hose tip onto the valve for a few seconds and then check it with the gauge. If you have overfilled, release air from the tire. Depress the center pin of the valve stem with a fingernail or a tool—you should hear a steady hiss as compressed air jets forth from the overinflated tire. Release the air in small increments so as not to release too much air, checking the tire pressure often while lowering the tire pressure. Replace the valve stem. Repeat the process for each tire.

4. Use a tread-depth tire gauge every other month. Forget about the penny-in-the-tread trick. A tread depth gauge only costs a few dollars and is far more accurate. Measure the tread depth about 1 in. from each edge and then the center tread. They should all be the same or within 1/32 in. If they're not, it is time for new tires. Refer to the Pro tip on pages 250-251 for **Diagnosing tire problems** to find the problems other than wear.

5. Rotate your tires every 6,000 miles.

pro tips!

Diagnosing tire problems

Bad alignment

➤ **Vehicle is out of alignment, and its tires are rolling on their edges.** The car most likely pulled to the side, but the driver ignored it. Ignoring the problem was costly. The tires wore out faster, and the vehicle still needed alignment. If your tread is worn on one side, get your vehicle aligned ASAP.

WEAR ON
ONE SIDE

Underinflated tires

➤ **Underinflation is the most common tire wear problem.** The center tread puckers toward the rim because there's not enough pressure to keep it in contact with the road. So the full weight of the car rides on the edges. In addition to premature wear, low tire pressure causes excessive heat and possible blowouts. The owner of these tires never bothered to keep the tires inflated.

WEAR ON
OUTER EDGE

Overinflated tires

➤ **Although overinflated tires may give you slightly higher gas mileage, they can cause much more serious problems than they solve.** Overinflated tires carry the entire weight of the car on the middle portion of the tread. Only the center tread was in contact with the road. That's why the center tread wore more than the edges.

On wet roads, the center tread can't pump the water out to the sides (think of a squeegee with a bulge in the center). So they're more prone to hydroplaning (like water skiing) and also more likely to skid in a stop or in a turn, and blow out on hard bumps. The bottom line: Overinflation is costly and dangerous. Always follow the inflation pressures shown on the car, not the tires.

WEAR ON
CENTER

Front-wheel-drive cars

➤ **The front tires on front-wheel-drive cars carry a heavier load and perform more work (steering and braking).** So they wear faster than the rears. Rotating tires every 6,000 miles spreads the wear across all four tires. Skip it and you'll find yourself with two bald tires in the front and two halfway good tires in the rear. You'll lose about 25 percent of the tire set's life.

COMPLEXITY
Simple

MATERIALS
120-grit sandpaper
Heavy-duty cleaner
Scrub brush
Metallic spray paint
for plastic

Refurbish old plastic wheel covers

Most plastic wheel covers are painted. After a while, the paint peels and all those curb kisses gouge the plastic. You don't have to buy new wheel covers. Just refinish the old ones.

1. Start by scraping the peeled areas. Then feather the peeled edges with 120-grit sandpaper. Sand down high ridges on the gouges until they're level with the rest of the wheel cover.

2. Wash the wheel cover with heavy-duty cleaner and a scrub brush. Rinse and dry. Then paint the entire wheel cover with a metallic spray paint rated for plastic.

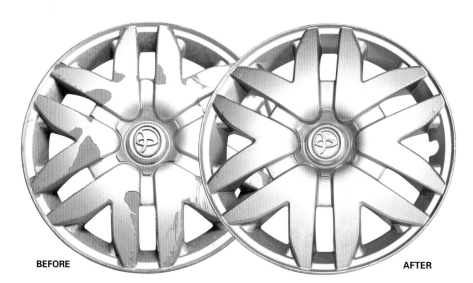

BEFORE   AFTER

pro tips!

➤ Newer plastic-type hubcaps and some wheel covers are usually held in place by a retaining wire ring that snaps into tabs on the wheel. When re-installing such a cap or cover, take care that you do not bend or break the tabs. Check to make sure they look even and flush.

pro tips!

Add pizzazz with bright-colored peelable paint

➤ **Peelable paint is the latest craze.** Car buffs use it to protect their wheel covers and rocker panels over the winter months or to give their rides a shot of color. Peelable paint is a spray-on rubbery coating that peels off when you're done with it. If you scratch it, you can simply recoat it.

➤ **When you use peelable paint outdoors, it should be removed after three months.** You can leave it on longer, but it'll be harder (or impossible) to remove.

➤ **Peelable paint is available at auto parts stores, home centers and craft stores.** Rust-Oleum, Dupli-Color and Plasti Dip are three well-known brands of peelable paint.

Clean dim headlights

PROFESSIONAL COST: $75

YOUR COST: $25

SAVINGS: $50

COMPLEXITY
Simple

MATERIALS
Headlight restoration kit

Road grit and the sun's UV rays can really do a number on your headlights. The grit literally blasts off the factory-applied protective coating, and the sun takes care of whatever coating is left. Then the lenses cloud over, dramatically reducing the amount of light they project. You've got two choices to see clearly again. You can either restore the old headlights with a restoration kit and a spare hour, or spend $40 to $250 each on new headlights. Tough choice, huh?

1. Before you buy a kit, check the headlight to see if the wear is on the outside of the lens. If you see moisture droplets on the inside of the lens or hairline cracks, the problem is on the inside and the headlight can't be restored. If it looks and feels like frosted glass, the restoration will probably work.

2. Shop smart—buy a complete headlight restoration kit. The kit should include tape to mask off the headlight, clear-coat remover (activator), sandpaper, polishing compound and cloths, gloves and a bottle of UV-block clear coat.

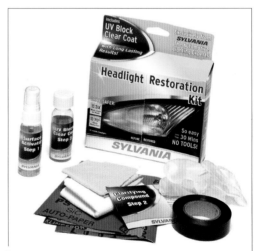

2

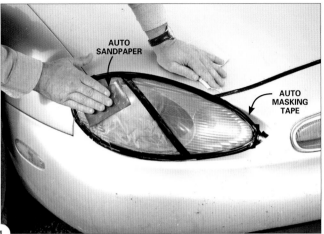

3. Start by masking off the areas around the headlight to prevent paint damage. Then apply the "activator" solution to soften any remaining clear coat. Wipe the lens clean.

4. Next, wet-sand the lens, starting with the coarsest sandpaper, and work your way to the finest grit. Apply some elbow grease. Wet-sand the lens in a circular pattern with medium pressure. Rewet the lens frequently with clear water.

5. Dry the lens and then polish the surface with the clarifying compound and the polishing cloth.

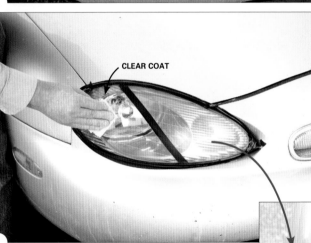

6. Clean off all the polishing compound and make sure the lens is dry before you apply the new clear coat. Wipe on the clear coat and let it dry for four to six hours before driving.